Kathryn Lamb

Is Anyone's Family as MAD as Mine?

A Survival Guide for Teenagers

PICCADILLY PRESS • LONDON

This edition published 2006
First published in Great Britain in 1997 by Piccadilly Press Ltd,
5 Castle Road,
London
NW1 8PR

A catalogue record for this book is available from the British Library.

ISBN: 1 85340 883 2 (trade paperback)
ISBN-13: 9 781853 408830

1 3 5 7 9 10 8 6 4 2

Printed and bound in Great Britain by Bookmarque Ltd.
Typeset by M Rules, London
Cover design by Simon Davis and Sue Hellard
Set in Bembo, Futura and Pike

Contents

Introduction

Wouldn't it be useful to have a resident Agony Aunt in your family, sitting in the corner, quietly observing what goes on, and dispensing advice? (Perhaps you already have one.) In fact, it would probably drive you mad and you would soon be asking her to leave, and go and solve her own problems.

What you really need (yes, really) is this book. Then, when your family's problems all get too much for you, you can tell them to go away and leave you in peace.

CAN'T YOU SEE I'M TRYING TO READ?!

And if you're feeling really stressed, you can always throw the book across the room (which you can't do with an Agony Aunt).

LIKE ALL MY PROBLEMS ARE SOOO SOLVED! NOT...

ANSWER: I Love You, Says I made you...

Who's that boy?/Who's that girl?

Here are the main characters you will meet:

• Angelica Toogood

Angelica is nearly fifteen, and comes from a nuclear family, which means she has two parents, called Mr and Mrs Toogood (surprisingly).

Mr Toogood is an accountant. He understands money, but he doesn't altogether understand where it goes now that he has a teenage daughter. Mrs Toogood looks after the house and does some charity work.

Angelica has one older brother, Grant, who is studying

THE TOOGOOD FAMILY

hard to get into university. Angelica finds him a bit strange as he hardly ever goes out – he prefers to stay in with a good book or to watch *Star Wars* DVDs.

Angelica also has a younger sister, Becky, who is eleven. Becky's main object in life is to invade her older sister's bedroom, try out her make-up, read her diary and borrow some of her clothes.

The Toogood family has a dog called Horace and a cat called Stanley.

• Danny Broke

Danny is fourteen and he's an only child, whose parents are divorced. He lives with his mother, Mrs Broke. He is

THE BROKE FAMILY

therefore the Single Child of a Single Parent. But every other weekend he goes to stay with his father, Mr Broke, who has married again. His father's new wife, whom Danny calls Sienna (since that is her name) has her own children: Leonora (eight), Theodora (six), Henrietta (four) and William (two). Danny's father and Sienna have now had a baby, called Henry.

Danny has mixed feelings about going to stay with his dad, as his step-sisters and step-brother (not to mention Henry) make loads of noise and Danny finds it hard to get enough sleep. He gets on well enough with his father, although he finds it difficult to get close to him (there is usually a step-brother or a step-sister, or even a howling

MR BROKE'S SECOND FAMILY

Henry the half-brother, in the way), and he blames his father for the fact that his mother is always broke and has to leave him for long periods while she is at work (in a fish shop). He forgets that she was broke even when she was married to Mr Broke.

His step-mother is not a wicked step-mother in the traditional fairy tale sense. Occasionally she is wicked in the sense of 'wonderful', for instance when she helped persuade Mr Broke to pay for Danny's saxophone lessons.

• Soumik Sen

Soumik is an only child with two doting parents who

THE SEN FAMILY

have high expectations of their son. Mr Sen wants
Soumik to join and eventually take over the family
business, importing rugs. What Mr Sen does not fully
appreciate is that Soumik wants to be a rock singer and
form his own band.

Soumik comes from a close-knit family, and there are
frequent family gatherings of all the various relations,
including Soumik's four cousins, three of whom are
girls. This means that Soumik finds himself the focus of
everyone's attentions, not all welcome. His girl cousins
tend to giggle a lot, and he is not always sure why they
are laughing. He hopes they will not be coming to his
concerts when he is famous.

THE CASH FAMILY

• Sam Cash

Sam is fifteen. The Cash family has a lot of cash (how did you guess?), and Sam enjoys spending it. His bedroom looks like the interior of a hi-fi and home cinema shop, there is so much equipment – all top of the range stuff. He plays the latest addition to his massive CD collection at full volume, often upsetting the neighbours. He also upsets the neighbours when he chases (and sometimes catches) their daughters. He thinks he is pretty cool, and wears cool shades all the time, even at breakfast (which means he has difficulty seeing if his toast is burnt, or how much Marmite he has spread on it).

Mr and Mrs Cash are both busy with their thriving careers, running their own businesses and making more and more cash. In fact, they are too busy to notice Sam.

Sam has a younger brother, James, who is thirteen. James admires Sam very much and wants to be like him. They are beginning to be known to the neighbours as 'those Cash brothers', or, in one word, trouble.

• Amy Average

Amy is fourteen. Her little brother Alex, aged eight, is known to Amy as 'Pest'. Mr Average was made redundant from his job as under-manager at a ladies' underwear factory, which means that the Average family no longer gets the free sets of matching bras and knickers which Mr Average used to bring home as a company perk. It also means they are relying on Mrs Average's income to support the family while Mr Average looks for a new job (there is not much demand for under-managers with

THE AVERAGE FAMILY

twenty years' experience in ladies' underwear). The family derives its income from Mrs Average's job as music teacher at the primary school which Alex attends.

The Average family has a parrot called Squawk.

These families are all different, but they have one thing in common (and most probably they have it in common with your family as well) – they all have problems.

CHAPTER 1
The Family at Home

PROBLEM 1: Parents in general

Parents have a tendency to worry. This makes them ask persistent, difficult or even downright impossible questions like, 'Are you all right?' (No), 'What are you doing?' (Nothing), 'What do you want to do when you leave school?' (Haven't really thought about it), 'Where are you going?' (Out), 'Who was that girl/boy?' (Which girl/boy?), 'What have you got there?' (Nothing), 'Have you done your homework?' (Not yet), 'Have you tidied your room?' (Yes, several months ago), and so on.

How do you deal with all these questions? There are good answers and bad answers. Basically, the good answers will get the persistent parent problem off your back, while the bad answers will cause parental anxiety, resulting in further awkward questions. So, if you just want peace and harmony all around, consider your answers carefully.

QUESTION 1: Are you all right?

• The scene

Amy Average has had a bad day. She has broken up with her best friend, Angelica Toogood, since Angelica said that the boy Amy fancies at school has bad breath, at least six fillings, one broken tooth, a spot on his tongue and enlarged tonsils. So Amy and Angelica have had a massive falling-out, and Amy is now at home, slumped in a chair in front of the TV, feeling too fed-up to move or even finish the open bag of Monster Crunch on her lap.

Mr and Mrs Average come into the room to watch *The Six O'Clock News*. They look at their daughter and they both say, together, 'Are you all right, Amy?' What reply should Amy give?

• Bad answer: 'No.' It may be quite obvious that this is the correct answer, but it is a bad answer to give if you just want to be left alone, because it will inevitably lead to further questions on matters you may prefer not to discuss. Does Amy really want to even try to explain to Mr and Mrs Average how Angelica came to notice that a boy at school has a spot on his tongue and enlarged tonsils? Or why it matters, anyway?

• **Good answer:** 'No, I broke up with my best friend.' A brief explanation like this may forestall further questions. They may ask, 'Why?' but you can say that you are too upset to talk about it. A caring parent will then make a noise expressing sympathy (or they may just be clearing their throat, it is sometimes hard to tell). You could ask them a whole battery of questions about the garden, their hobbies, work, etc. In other words, distract them.

• **Even better answer:** 'Yes, I'm fine.' No further questions, M'Lud (unless it's very, very obvious you're not OK).

QUESTION 2: What are you doing?

• The scene

Danny is chilling out on the sofa, watching a *Star Wars* DVD. His mother asks, 'What are you doing?'

• Bad answer – 1: 'Nothing.' The obvious answer is

very often the bad answer. There is nothing more likely to irritate a parent than the sight of their offspring doing 'nothing'. Nothing very constructive or purposeful, that is. You have to be doing 'something' useful or intelligent in order to satisfy your parent.

• Bad answer – 2: 'Just chilling, Mum.' This answer

is quite likely to cause irritation, too. Your parent may have a curious vision of you sitting on a shelf in the chilled foods section of the supermarket. Most parents will just get annoyed because 'chilling' is just another way of saying you are doing 'nothing'.

• Slightly better answer: 'Thinking.' Your parent will

feel greatly encouraged by the news that your brain is in full working order, and that you are capable of thought. However, the vagueness of this answer may cause them to wonder what you are thinking about, and the question, 'What are you thinking about?' is just as potentially difficult as, 'What are you doing?'

• Good answer: 'I'm thinking about what I should

put in my essay on the socio-ecological implications of

sending dogs into cyberspace. It has to be in by Thursday. This programme is really helpful.' An answer like this should silence them completely. In other words, give your parent an answer which not only indicates that your

brain is still working, but also indicates that you are hyper-intelligent and your mind is likely to be teeming with all sorts of concepts well beyond the grasp of the average parent. So they will say, 'Ah!' and nod their heads thoughtfully. Then, with any luck, they will leave you to it and tiptoe away, and you can continue watching your DVD in peace.

The Family at Home

QUESTION 3: What do you want to do when you leave school?

• The scene
The Toogood family is discussing the projected brilliant career in international banking which their son Grant has decided he wishes to pursue. Mr Toogood then turns to his daughter Angelica and inquires gently, 'And what do you want to be, Angel?' (He manages to stop himself, just in time, from adding the words, 'when you grow up'.)

• Bad answer – 1: 'Haven't really thought about it.'
The average parent will retort, 'Well it's about time you did.'

• Bad answer – 2: 'Sam says there's this really cool commune in Wales where they live in abandoned cowsheds and just eat nuts and berries, and it's, er … great. I might go and join them.' Your parents will be horrified at the thought of you getting mixed up with anything 'alternative', especially if it is on the recommendation of a friend of whom they do not approve.

• Bad answer – 3: 'Well, one thing's for certain – I don't want to be an accountant.' It would be more tactful to say something like: 'I don't think I have the tremendous dedication and patience necessary to be an accountant like you.' And try not to reel off endless lists of things you don't want to be. This can get boring.

• **Bad answer – 4:** 'I want to be an actor/artist/lead singer with a rock band.' Unless you have such enormous talent that you have already won a scholarship to drama school or sold your paintings for thousands of pounds to an American buyer, your parents are likely to be worried because you are choosing a career with no real financial security. And as for 'lead singer with a rock band', they will immediately think 'sex, drugs, alcohol, strange hair', and the warning bells will sound so loudly in their heads that they will be heard by the neighbours all the way down the street.

• **Good answer – 1:** 'I want to train to be a lawyer.' Or it could be any profession or trade (nurse/doctor/architect/vet/bricklayer/teacher, etc), but the important thing is that you should train for it. Your parents have been trying for years to train you to be a normal, sensible member of the human race, and they will be reassured to think that you will be carrying on with the training in the future. (They have also tried to train the dog, and totally failed, but it is kind to let them think they have been more successful with you.)

• **Good answer – 2:** 'I want to be an accountant/be a successful business person like you, Mum/Dad.' A flattering answer like this, and an apparent wish to follow in the parental footsteps (Angelica's father is an accountant) will delight them.

• **Good answer – 3:** 'I want to work in Active-X

21

HTML layout.' No one quite knows what this means, but it sounds impressive.

QUESTION 4: Where are you going?

• The scene

Angelica wants to go out for a walk in the hope that she might see Sam, whom she fancies. She knows her parents don't approve of Sam, so she is trying to slip out through the door without them noticing. She should know better. No sooner does she open the front door than her mum says, 'Where are you going?' (Or 'Where do you think *you're* going?', which is a more provocative way of asking the same question – likely to provoke a less than polite response.)

• Bad answer: 'Out.' Again, the obvious answer is the bad one, but it is also the vagueness of the answer which raises suspicion and causes anxiety – and the abruptness of the answer sounds rude and is likely to cause offence.

• Good answer: 'I'm going out for a walk. I need some fresh air before I get on with my homework.' This brief explanation gives reassurance that you are going out for the most straightforward and healthiest of reasons, and also carries the added reassurance that you will soon be back, again for the best of reasons (to get on with your homework).

WHERE DO
YOU THINK
YOU'RE
GOING ?

• **Even better answer:** 'I'm going to the shop. I need another pad of paper for my history homework. Would you like anything while I'm there?' This is a good answer if it is obvious your parent is on the point of saying you can't go out. You will see a thought bubble appear above their head and into it will float a loaf of bread or some other essential item which they would quite like from the shop. So they will send you off to get it, and they may even give you some money and tell you to keep the change (or not, depending on how stingy they are).

• **Good answer which goes too far:** 'I'm going out for a walk. Shall I take the dog?' Angelica gives this answer and her mum instantly says, 'Oh, yes, what a good idea! I think I'll come too!' Fantastic. Not.

• **Over-neat answer:** 'I'm just going over to Robbie's house to borrow an envelope.' It sounds plausible but your family will probably stare at you and say, 'But we've got loads of envelopes!' You will then find yourself having to add on bits to the original excuse, making it sound more and more unlikely, such as, 'But I need a certain *kind* of envelope which only Robbie has.'

• **Over-honest answer:** 'Me and Amy are going out stalking guys.' Such brutal honesty will do nothing to restore parental confidence. Try watering it down slightly for parental consumption, for example: 'Amy and I (correct grammar makes you sound grown-up and responsible) are going to admire the view/local beauty spot/stars.' You could even take a telescope or pair of binoculars with you, through which you could admire the 'view' (local talent). In other words, give an answer which leaves room for manoeuvre.

QUESTION 5: Where have you been?

• **The scene**
Angelica has managed to slip out on her own without either the dog or her mother, but she has not seen Sam, despite trying all the places he usually hangs out, so she has returned home disappointed, rather later than even she had expected. She tries to slink up to her room silently, unnoticed.

'Where have you been?' (Or: 'Where do you think *you've* been?' – as if you are seriously deluded and given to imagining you've been somewhere when you haven't.)

• **Bad answer:** 'Out.' The shortness and vagueness of this kind of answer is what gets you into trouble, especially if you are acting furtively. Your parents will think you have something to hide.

- **Even worse answer:** 'I *think* I've been out.' This is guaranteed to cause Parental Apoplexy, which is a truly terrible condition.

WHERE
HAVE
YOU
BEEN?

- **Good answer:** 'I had a good, long walk. It's a really beautiful evening. The birds are singing, and I glimpsed a flight of wild ducks winging their way overhead as I strolled through the park. Now I feel totally refreshed, and ready to get on with my homework.' All right, so this answer is a little O.T.T. But any kind of cheerful, upbeat response will do the trick. No further questions.

QUESTION 6: Who was that girl/boy?

• The scene

Mr Average has come to collect Amy from school. He finds her in the school playground chatting to the boy she fancies (and trying to see if it is true what Angelica said, that he has six fillings, a spot on his tongue and enlarged tonsils). On the way home in the car, Mr Average says, 'Who was that boy?'

• Bad answer: 'Which boy?' It will always irritate a parent when you answer a question with a question. What they are looking for is an answer, and even if you feel that it is none of their business, it is unwise to treat them as though they are stupid. It must be obvious which boy they are referring to, unless you have recently (say in the last fifteen minutes) chatted up every boy in the school playground. What are you trying to hide?

• Good answer: 'That was Matthew.' If you have a particularly persistent parent problem, they may want to know more about Matthew. So try an:

• Even better answer: 'That was Matthew. He's in my class. I was asking him about our geography home-work.' This is a sufficiently boring answer to render the whole subject of 'Which boy?' (Matthew) totally dead. They will then leave you in peace to dream about Matthew to your heart's content.

QUESTION 7: What have you got there?

• The scene

Danny's girlfriend has given him a little heart-shaped box with a lock of her hair in it. Danny has just come home and is sitting in the dark in the living-room watching TV, opening and closing the box. It makes a little snapping noise each time he closes it. Suddenly his mother appears in the doorway. 'What have you got there?' she asks.

• Bad answer: 'Nothing.' If it is perfectly obvious that you have something in your hand/behind your back/ up your shirt, it is better not to pretend that you haven't.

WHAT HAVE
YOU GOT THERE?

• Good answer: 'It's a little box.' A matter-of-fact answer, which also happens to be true, should satisfy your parent's inquiring mind. He or she may, of course (as

Danny's mother did) say, 'What's inside it?' If you would prefer your parent not to take a closer look at whatever it is, try to put them off with an:

• Even better answer: 'It's a little box, and I've got a rather interesting spider inside it.' This is an answer designed to put most mothers off. Try to think of something harmless but horrid, or deadly dull, in which your parents cannot possibly be interested.

QUESTION 8: Have you done your homework?

• The scene
Angelica Toogood is lying on her bed, studying the latest article about her favourite group, Gobsmackers, in a magazine. Mr Toogood puts his head round the door and asks, 'Have you done your homework?'

• Bad answer: 'Not yet.' This is a particularly bad answer if it is eleven p.m. and everyone is just going to bed.

• Slightly better answer: 'Not yet. But I haven't got to hand it in tomorrow. I've got till Thursday. I'll get on with it now/tomorrow/soon.'

• Much better answer: 'Yes.' In fact, this is the only answer that will really satisfy the average parent.

• **Brilliant answer:** 'Yes. Would you like to read my essay on the socio-ecological implications of the fast food industry? It's only twenty pages long.' Most parents will suddenly find they have something very urgent to do downstairs.

• **Alternative brilliant answer:** 'Not yet. Amy and I are doing a geography project together, so I need to go over to her house tomorrow evening to get on with it.' This is an excellent excuse for Angelica to go to Amy's house where they can read magazines together. (And do their homework.)

QUESTION 9: Have you tidied your room?

This question is sometimes phrased differently, such as, 'Have you seen your room recently?' (This is silly. *Of course* you've seen it. But it is not a good idea to point out the logical gaps in your parents' thought processes.)

• **The scene**

Angelica has just come downstairs from a room which looks as though several herds of stampeding elephants have just passed through it. Mrs Toogood asks, 'Have you tidied your room recently?' Here is a list of possible answers to an impossible question:

• **Bad answer:** 'I like my room the way it is. Besides,

I know where everything is.' This is especially bad if you are always losing things.

• **Slightly better answer:** 'The untidiness of my room is only superficial. It is expressive of a complex personality, and masks an inner beauty and structure which are only apparent to those with the true poetic vision. I happen to be a wild and free, creative spirit who soars above the everyday banalities of life, such as tidying my room.' This is quite a difficult answer to remember and it will leave your parent seething with irritation. It is probably in your best interest to give:

• **The only really good answer:** 'Yeah, I know it's a mess, but I want to finish some homework first.' You can run this one for a maximum of three days.

Here are another two impossible parental questions/ remarks, with some possible answers:

QUESTION/REMARK 10: You can't possibly go out looking like that! You're a mess!

Now, this may or may not be true, but it's obviously very rude of them to say so. How would they like it if someone told them they were a complete mess? But losing your temper will achieve nothing. Instead, count to ten and consider the following answers:

• **Quite good answer:** 'But Mum, it's The Look! I've spent hours making myself look like this. In fact, if I don't look like this, my friends will laugh at me and say I'm a complete idiot.'

• **Not so good answer:**

IF YOU THINK I'M A MESS, YOU SHOULD SEE THE PEOPLE I'M ABOUT TO GO OUT WITH?!

• **Very bad answer:** 'You don't look so hot yourself.'

• **Truly inspired answer:** 'Yes, I know I'm a mess. I've grown out of all my clothes, and I'm really upset because I've got nothing to wear. I can't even afford a haircut. My friends will laugh at me unless ... (pause a few seconds for full effect) ... unless you'd be really kind and give me some money so I can go out and get some nice new clothes!' You might even shed a few tears at this point, depending on how much of a soft touch your parent is.

And finally:

BEFORE
(COOL)

AFTER YOUR
MOTHER HAS
RUN A COMB
THROUGH
YOUR HAIR
(UNCOOL)

BEFORE
(I HATE MY
HAIR!)

AFTER
(THAT'S
BETTER!)

QUESTION/REMARK 11: Haven't you forgotten something?

Here is a list of things you might have forgotten:

1) Mum's birthday/Dad's birthday/Gran's birthday/ Grandad's birthday/Uncle Derek's birthday/your own birthday (unlikely). If this question suddenly reminds you

WINNING SMILES

of what you have forgotten, say hastily that you haven't forgotten, really, and you're just about to phone whoever it is, or go out and get them a card/present.

2) To say 'Please' or 'Thank you'. A winning smile, a big 'Thank you' or 'Please' will get you out of this one. Winning smiles are hard. Practise them every night before you go to bed.

3) What else might you have forgotten? To do your homework? To get dressed? To hug/kiss your parent fondly and say 'Goodbye' (regardless of the fact that you will be seeing them several hours later)? To feed the gerbils? Actually, the list of possibilities is endless. Try apologising and saying something like: 'I have a memory like a sieve. Please remind me.' In other words, be polite, and remember: a happy parent is a kind and generous parent.

If you really want their approval and their support for your latest idea or venture, keep them happy. Let's begin with a few ideas for keeping a mother happy.

KEEPING A MOTHER HAPPY

• Method 1
Be considerate. Remember that your mother may not relish all the washing and housework as much as the happy housewife portrayed in TV and magazine ads. She may well go out to work during the day (like Danny's

mother, Mrs Broke, who works in a fishmonger's), in order to earn some money to pay the bills (financial necessity), and sometimes in order to stimulate her mind so that she comes home to you refreshed and feeling more alive. Except, of course, that she may also be feeling quite tired after a hard day's work at the office/on the farm/at the fishmonger's/flying the helicopter or whatever. So the last thing she really needs when she comes through the door is to be confronted by an enormous heap of dirty washing, ironing, and a kitchen full of unwashed coffee mugs, dirty plates, etc, and the dog, cat, parrot all whining, meowing and squawking at her because no one has bothered to feed them.

• **The wrong approach:** If Danny Broke, for instance, chooses this moment to say, 'What's for supper, Mum?' he is likely to get a fairly short answer. ('Fish' is actually the answer.)

There is certainly not much hope of Mrs Broke agreeing to iron his favourite smart shirt (which has been stuffed under his bed since the last time he wore it), and giving him some money so he can go out with a friend straight after supper. Danny needs to get his act together a bit, and try:

• **The right approach:** Help with the chores. After greeting his mother warmly when she gets home from work, Danny offers to help clear up the mess which is everywhere. Better still, he will already have done this before Mrs Broke got home. And if he really wants to go rocketing heavenwards in his mother's estimation,

Danny will tell her to sit down and put her feet up while he gets her a cup of coffee/tea/something stronger, and then gets on with the washing-up or does some of the ironing. She will think of him as a dream son, and when he eventually asks, 'What's for supper, Mum?' she is likely to say, 'Fish'. (Ah well, some things never change.) However, she is much more likely to agree to iron his clothes, and to give him some money so he can go out, on condition that he is back by a certain time. This is quite reasonable, and if he makes sure that he is back by a certain time, she is more likely to say, 'Yes' the next time, and the time after that.

• Method 2

Remind her of when you were a baby. This works for Soumik Sen every time. He brings out the cherished family album, stuffed with photos of baby Soumik, with his huge melting dark brown eyes, and cheeky smile. 'Look, Mother, here is Soumik lying on a rug with nothing on!' He also has to make sure that the family-size box of Kleenex is to hand, as the sight of her sweet baby Soumik never fails to reduce Mrs Sen to tears as the fond memories crowd in. He is still her baby! She will do almost anything for him. He only has to ask.

• What Mrs Sen is likely to say: 'Yes.'

However, this tactic tends to backfire when the cherished family album is brought out on family occasions and shown to Soumik's girl cousins. Then there is much giggling, and pointing at the photos of Soumik with nothing

OH, SOUMIK — YOU HAVEN'T CHANGED MUCH!

on, and comments such as, 'Oh, Soumik, you haven't changed much!'

• Method 3

Flattery. Soumik also finds that his mother is very amenable and likely to support his cause if he pays her a compliment. Danny has discovered that this works well with Mrs Broke, too. But again, there is a Right Approach and a Wrong Approach to paying a compliment.

• The wrong approach: 'Your hair looks nice, Mum, can I have ten pounds?'

OH, HI, MUM — YOU'RE LOOKING REALLY GREAT TODAY — WOULD YOU IRON A FEW SHIRTS FOR ME ?

• **The right approach:** It works much better if you really take the time and trouble to notice that she has had her hair done, or is wearing a new dress, and you tell her how nice she looks. After all, you like it, too, when she notices that you have gone to a lot of trouble with your appearance, and pays you a compliment.

Be kind.

Be tactful.

And remember that your mother could be one of the best friends you'll ever have, and she will most certainly be one of your greatest admirers! So now we have cheered up your mother (have we?), how about Dad? Here are a few suggestions for lifting the spirits (and opening the wallet!) of a depressed dad:

KEEPING A FATHER HAPPY

• The scene – 1
Amy Average certainly wants her father to feel happy because she wants him to drive her and Angelica to the Gobsmackers concert at the stadium in New Borehampton on Saturday.

• What she hopes he will say: 'Yes! Certainly, I'll drive you to the Gobsmackers concert at the stadium in New Borehampton on Saturday. It's only eighty miles away, and most of that is motorway. The car needs a good run. Of course I'll lend you the money for the tickets! Good heavens, are they as much as that? Well, never mind, let's hope it's a good evening!'

However, the prospects of her father saying any such thing are remote as Amy enters the room and sees him slumped in an armchair, looking totally depressed, and watching the news, which is making him feel even more depressed.

• The wrong approach: 'Hi, Dad. Can I have some money for the Gobsmackers concert at the stadium in New Borehampton on Saturday, and will you drive me and Angelica there, and collect us later?' He is likely to say: 'No.'

• **The right approach - 1:** Flattery (again). Amy tells Mr Average how much she enjoys it when he comes to her school to collect her in the car, because all her friends, especially Angelica, think he's dishy. Since Mr Average is short and bespectacled, with a receding hairline and advancing waistline, he looks faintly surprised, but at the same time pleased. He *wants* to believe his daughter.

• **The right approach - 2:** Straightforward affection. Amy gives Mr Average a big hug and tells him she loves him loads, and he's the best dad in the world. She is *still* his little girl, and she can twist him around her little finger. It is a good idea to show him that she really *does* care, and respect his feelings. In other words, it is probably *not* a good idea to have her head shaved (all her pretty curls – gone!) and to dress entirely in black, including a

ALL HER PRETTY HAIR - GONE!

pair of heavy boots, if she wishes him to feel indulgent towards his 'little girl'.

A little bit of consideration in her approach to her father, and he is more likely to say, 'Yes, all right, I'll take you and Angelica to the Gobsmackers concert, but I think I'd better come with you, to make sure that my favourite daughter is all right.'

Amy's jaw is likely to sag at the thought of sitting next to her father at the Gobsmackers concert. This is a father whose idea of music is singing along to opera in his bath, and who objects if anyone turns up the volume on the sound system when his favourite late night (ten-thirty p.m.) Singalonga Something Simple programme is on Radio 2. But it is better, she may conclude, than not going at all. Anyway, if she goes totally hyper at the concert, at least her father will be there to catch her when she passes out.

• The scene - 2
Danny goes to stay with his father and step-family every other weekend. It is very difficult to talk to his father about anything because there is nearly always a small step-brother or step-sister in the way, or a howling Henry the half-brother. So what does he do, in order to get some time on his own with his dad, in a quiet, relaxed atmosphere?

• The wrong approach: Being cross. 'For God's sake, Dad, can't a guy get any peace round here? Who cares, anyway? You don't seem to, so why should I? You don't even want to talk to me. You can't even hear me.'

This is a somewhat negative approach, since a lack of

opportunity for Danny and his father to get together and have a quiet chat does not amount to the same thing as not wanting to.

• The right approach: Being considerate. They should both try to find a point of contact, an activity they can do on their own together, away from the rest of the family, even if it is just a country walk, or a mooch around the shops and cafés. (Some dads have been known to mooch quite well.)

• What Danny hopes his father will say: 'OK, son, I'll take you out for the day. We'll go bowling at the Hyper Bowl, then we'll take in a film at the Multiplex, and I'll get you the new skateboard I know you want, and we'll end our day with a slap-up meal at

The Blue Porcupine' (another exciting, expensive, happenin' place, with all-night dancing and a live jazz band which Danny admires very much because he is learning to play the saxophone).

• **What Danny's father actually says:** 'I think we'll go fishing.' This is about the last thing Danny really wants to do. He *hates* fish. It is bad enough having a mother who works at a fishmonger's and who comes home every day smelling of fish. They have to eat fish every single night because his mother gets it free from the

I THINK I'VE GOT SOMETHING, DANNY MY BOY — YES! IT'S A FISH!

fishmonger's, which saves on the housekeeping. And now, as if to add insult to injury, his father proposes to take him *fishing*. It is as though his whole life revolves around fish, and he cannot get away from it.

At least he will have some time on his own with his father and an opportunity to talk about other things (apart from fish). Sometimes a companionable silence is just as good. It is not always necessary to say anything.

If you're lucky, it is often enough just to know that your father is there for you.

Finally, here is a list of things you should definitely not say to your parents:

1) 'Sam's really into body piercing. He says it's cool. What do you guys think about it? I'm thinking of getting my nipples done.'

Avoid saying anything which starts with, 'Sam says …' when you know that your parents can't stand the sight of Sam (or Matthew, or Jez, or whoever it might be). Also, don't ask your parents' opinion on a subject and then just carry on talking without giving them a chance to reply, or offer you their advice. This will cause them great annoyance and frustration, and they will not feel kindly disposed towards you next time you ask for anything. And avoid using words like 'nipples' at the dinner table.

2) 'There's a really good diet in this magazine, Dad. You can lose two kilos in a week by eating the right combination of carbohydrate and protein one day, and nothing at all the next except for one medium-sized cucumber. You really ought to try it, Dad. You need to.'

A little gentle teasing is all right, but go steady. Don't overdo it. Put yourself in his shoes (yes, I know you'd look pretty silly in his shoes!) and imagine how you'd feel on the receiving end of such remarks.

And so you retreat to the sanctuary of your own room, where you can put on your favourite music and settle down to consider:

PROBLEM 2: How to co-exist with the rest of your family

You know how it is. You all have to live in the same house. So how do you get on with your nearest and dearest (or simply your nearest)? There are certain family rituals which have to be respected, if you are all going to keep your health and temper.

FAMILY MEALTIMES

• The scene – 1

Mrs Toogood has been busy in the kitchen most of the day. She has baked seventeen amazing ginger and gooseberry cakes, and is now slaving over her family's supper, which is bubbling away furiously on top of the cooker. She has been to a lot of trouble with the preparation of the supper, and a lot of carefully prepared ingredients (including eight cloves of garlic, a litre of red wine, twelve shallots, two red peppers and ten lightly fried wings of duck) have gone into it. Clouds of steam are billowing from the open kitchen door and out through the open window, and the perspiration is dripping from Mrs Toogood's nose and back into the enormous saucepan as she gives the supper one final stir before summoning her family to the table. She hopes they are hungry.

• The wrong approach: Angelica bursts into the kitchen through the billowing clouds of steam. 'Oh, Mum,' she says, 'I don't want any supper. I pigged out on three Mars bars and a packet of Demon Crunch on the bus coming home, and I feel sick. By the way, can you lend me your white jacket?'

Behind Angelica is Becky. 'Hi, Mum,' she says, 'I don't want any supper. I'm trying this amazing lettuce sandwich and Mars bar diet. It really works, you know? Oh, and I need five pounds to buy a new top from New Look. I lost the other one you got me.'

Well, what can I say? Both girls should instantly be reported to the S.P.C.M. (Society for the Prevention of Cruelty to Mothers). There is no chance that either of them will get what they want, anyway. And Mr Toogood and Grant will be eating spicy duck wings for the next few days.

• The right approach: This time Angelica enters the kitchen inhaling deeply. Mrs Toogood's hair has now gone frizzy in the steam from the bubbling saucepans. 'What a wonderful smell!' she cries. 'Your hair looks nice, Mum! And that looks delicious! Mmmm! I'm really hungry.'

Even if not a word of this is true (especially not the 'Mmmm!'), it creates the right atmosphere in which she can eat some of her supper and quietly dispose of what's left while the rest of the Toogood family are hypnotised by the TV. Her mother will also agree to lend her the white jacket (which Angelica wants to wear later this evening when she goes to see Sam).

Becky can follow the example of her elder sister, forget dieting and say something nice about the supper instead. Then she might get her new top.

Occasionally, Mrs Toogood wonders why the Toogood

dog, Horace, is so fat. The reason for this is simple enough. Mr Toogood has been feeding him surreptitiously under the table, and the girls have also been sneaking him titbits.

Offer to cook the supper yourself occasionally, and consider how offended you'd feel if the whole family declined to eat what you'd worked so hard to prepare. You wouldn't want to do anything for them after that, would you?

ANGELICA ACQUIRES THE 'LINDSAY LOHAN' LOOK (HAIR, MAKEUP, STAR QUALITY ETC.)

• The scene – 2

For many a teenager, the family dinner table is less a focus of interest than the fridge. There is a strange magnetic attraction between the average teenager and the fridge. Forget fridge magnets. Just look, and you'll see a teenager apparently stuck to the fridge, or a little group of teenagers all huddled around it, inspecting its contents. Angelica Toogood, Danny Broke and Soumik Sen carry

MORE FRIDGE MAGNET THAN BABE MAGNET

out routine inspections of their parents' fridges at least ten times every day and night, and usually walk off with something interesting they have found inside them.

• **The wrong approach:** 'Mum!' cries Danny, in a deeply wounded tone of voice. 'There's nothing left in the fridge!'

• **What Danny's mother is likely to say:** 'That's because you've eaten it all! And I can't afford to go shopping again now till Tuesday. We'll have to make do with fish.'

• The right approach: It is only fair to ask a parent before you walk off with anything from the fridge. Otherwise, you might just have eaten the one essential ingredient for tonight's supper, or all of the cheese intended to last for the rest of the week. The more consideration you show towards the Parent Who Wears The Boots In The Kitchen (if you see what I mean), the more likely they are to indulge your particular tastes and cravings.

Another culinary don't:

Don't use the same knife, covered in marmalade, to spread Marmite straight from the pot, and butter from its wrapper and then spread some pâté, and finally, covered as it is by now with a strange mixture of Marmite and marmalade pâté, to cut yourself a portion of brie, straight from the fridge. Do not then leave the knife rather threateningly on the bread board, all covered in crumbs and God knows what. It will certainly frighten your father next time he goes to the bread board to prepare himself a slice of bread and butter.

YOUR OWN ROOM

Once the family meal is over, it is probably time to retreat once again to the peace and tranquillity of your own room. But just how peaceful and tranquil is it, in reality? Naturally, you want to keep it as a safe haven to retreat to when you have had enough of your family's delightful company and stimulating conversation. It is nice to be able to close the door (never slam it, no matter how cross you are – it might come off its hinges, and you would be lost without it!), and just be on your own with your thoughts and dreams, favourite music, magazines, etc.

• The scene

Angelica Toogood is feeling sick, having sampled a slice of her mother's latest cake creation, Kiwi and Cream with Cointreau Sponge Supreme. Horace the dog has just been sick on the carpet (perhaps he tried a slice of cake, too), and her father is in a bad mood, having found a patch of Angelica's Flossy Pink nail varnish on the arm of his favourite armchair, and a half-eaten packet of Beastly Crunch hidden under the cushion (it made a horrid noise when he sat down on it). And now Horace the dog has done something really terrible.

JUST DON'T ASK WHAT HE DID –
YOU DON'T WANT TO KNOW.

Angelica feels the need to get away from it all and be on her own for a while. She goes upstairs to her room and finds …

… Recurrent Family Pest Syndrome Number One, in the shape of her little sister, Becky, who is sitting at Angelica's dressing table, trying out all her make-up, and making a real mess of it. As far as Angelica can fathom, invading her older sister's bedroom and trying out her clothes and make-up seems to be Becky's sole intention in life. She also borrows Angelica's favourite CDs, without asking, reads her diary and goes off with her magazines. She persistently asks irritating questions, such as, 'What ya doing, Jelly?' (Angelica hates this name), 'Are you going anywhere tonight?', 'Can I come in?', 'Have you kissed him yet?' and, 'Do Mum and Dad know about this?' In other words, Becky might just tell Mum and Dad, unless Angelica gives her exactly what she wants. So what does Angelica do?

• **The wrong solution:** Angelica shouts, 'OUT! NOW!' at her little sister, and when Becky has gone she slams the door (bad mistake!), and piles furniture against it. This is all very well, but it now means that Angelica herself cannot get out of her room, even if she just wants to go to the bathroom. She is also aware that the Recurrent Family Pest Syndrome Number One is still outside her room, waiting. For some reason, Becky will not go to bed until Angelica does, even if it means propping her eyelids open with matchsticks in order to stay up.

• **The right solution:** Angelica could try to befriend her little sister. She could be 'nice' to her! A somewhat revolutionary approach, of course, but it might just work. Up to now, they have just wound each other up by doing things like borrowing each other's clothes without asking,

and Angelica has upset Becky by stretching her baby pink T-shirt out of shape with her 'enormous boobs'! Instead of carrying on like this, they could start by asking each other before they borrow anything. It is possible that Becky admires her older sister (well, anything is possible) and wants some attention. Angelica could give Becky some old make-up she no longer wants, and a few old magazines, maybe even a top she no longer wears, and say to her, 'Here, take these. I don't want them. You can take them into your room. I just want a bit of time on my own right now, OK, but you can come back when I call you and we'll listen to some music.' Becky will now be looking rather taken aback, but also quite pleased. This could be the start of a new and happy relationship, in which Becky and Angelica feel they can talk to each other in confidence, and respect each other's privacy. Also, the friendlier they are to each other, the happier and more relieved Mr and Mrs Toogood will be, and, as we all know, a happy parent is a kind and generous parent, a parent who likes to say yes!

(NOT) YOUR OWN ROOM

There is not so much chance of privacy if you happen to share a room with a sibling. In this situation, there are certain basic rules you should remember:

1) Don't play your Dr Drear and the Deadheads album at maximum volume if you know your sibling has a headache/prefers gentle piano or guitar music, played

SISTERLY LOVE

quietly. If your sibling is under six years of age, a massive dose of Dr Drear and the Deadheads will probably make him or her howl, and it will certainly elicit the classic parental war-cry up the stairs: 'TURN THAT NOISE DOWN AT ONCE!'

2) Don't cover every conceivable square centimetre of wall space with posters and pictures of Gob (lead singer with the Gobsmackers) if you know that your sibling can't stand the sight of him. It will only give your sibling nightmares/make him or her feel sick. Also, they might appreciate some wall space of their own, to cover with pictures of the object of their own desires. (Try not to worry too much if this turns out to be a horse. They will grow out of it. Probably.)

3) When you remove your trainers at the end of a long, hot day, remember to put them outside the bedroom door (but not too close to your parents' door). Remove your socks to a safe distance.

4) It is probably better to listen to music, especially if it is late at night, through your headphones. Don't sing along to it.

5) Don't sing at all, or make any other kind of anti-social or disturbing noise.

6) Don't snore, talk in your sleep or sleep-walk.

BATHROOM PROBLEMS

There is immediately a problem if you have only one bathroom, and more than one person living in the house. The problem is made worse if the loo and the bathroom are not separate, especially since the average teenage girl seems to believe that the bathroom belongs by rights to her, and she resents any intrusion into it by other members of the family, such as her father. She will hammer on the door if there is someone in the bathroom and shout: 'ARE YOU GOING TO BE LONG?' Other members of the family may have their own back on her later when they, in turn, hammer on the door and shout: 'FOR GOD'S SAKE, YOU'VE BEEN IN THERE THREE HOURS!

PRECIOUS 'ME-TIME'

WHAT ON EARTH ARE YOU DOING?' They know she must be all right, because they can hear all sorts of noises coming from inside the bathroom; splashing, gargling, occasional singing, and so on.

• The scene

Angelica has beaten everyone again in the general morning stampede for the bathroom. She has successfully occupied it, locked the door and set up camp inside it. Her intention this morning is to apply perfect make-up – each eyelash must be separated, coated and curled – in order to attract Sam. Her father knocks on the door. He has an important interview at the bank this morning, which may result in a promotion and pay-rise. He would like to have a shave. But time is ticking by.

• The wrong thing to do: Angelica does one eyelash at a time and keeps her father waiting. When he eventually gets into the bathroom, he finds mascara all over his shaving mirror, and the bathroom floor is all wet from the de-stressing lavender oil bath which Angelica had earlier.

• The right thing to do: Angelica should stop obsessing about her eyelashes and let her father have his shave. It is more important that he should go to his interview in the right frame of mind, with a clean shave, and get his promotion, which will be of enormous benefit to his family, including Angelica. It will be of no benefit to anyone if Angelica manages to attract Sam with her

separated and curled eyelashes. To her father she will just be a nuisance with great eyelashes, and he won't be feeling kindly or generously disposed towards her if she blocks his way to the bathroom.

TELEPHONE AND TV TROUBLES

You may feel that you could not possibly survive without your mobile, but there are times when other people probably feel that they could very happily live without it. Here are some examples of occasions when it might be a good idea to switch your mobile off:

1) Mealtimes. When your mum or dad (or it could be anyone!) has spent hours slaving over a hot oven to produce a meal (even if battered haddock is not your favourite and the peas are burned). It is not polite to talk on your phone while your food goes cold. Your parents in particular are likely to seethe and come to the boil (like the peas), and are unlikely to be able to contain their simmering rage if you keep shrieking 'Ohmigod!' into your phone while the food congeals on your plate.

2) At the cinema/theatre/brother or sister's school production/library – anywhere people are likely to turn round in their seats, fix you with a look of pure loathing and go 'Ssssh!!!'

3) School. Your phone will be confiscated, held to ransom – 'If you do me an eight-hundred-word essay on the lifecycle of the giant squid by Friday, you can have your phone back' or possibly destroyed by Mr Murgatroyd the mad resistant materials teacher who is on a mission to wipe out any material that dares to resist him.

4) Church/mosque/temple/monastic retreat any place of quiet meditation or prayer. This includes your sister's wedding ...

• The scene

Fast forward a number of years to Angelica's wedding to ... to ... a man named Bill. He is a nice man. But that's irrelevant. The fact is that Angelica has spent the last three years (it was a long engagement) scrimping and saving for her Big Day. NOTHING must ruin it! But

Becky the Bridesmaid has forgotten to switch off her phone, which is in the pretty flower basket which she has just carried up the aisle. She put it there absentmindedly when Angelica arrived at the church – she has never seen her sister look soo beautiful! The whole congregation is now hushed in awe as the marriage service takes place.

The vicar: 'Do you, Angelica Rosemary Violet Toogood, take this man, Bill [OK, he has other names but let's just get on with it] to be your lawful wedded husband?'

Angelica opens her mouth to reply but before the words 'I do' have a chance to leave her trembling lips, Becky's phone goes off loudly – her new ringtone is called 'Psycho' and features the scary music from the film of the same name, plus an additional features of insane, maniacal laughter, which echoes through the church. All eyes turn to stare (HARD STARE!) at Becky who fumbles for her phone, drops the flower basket and blushes fuschia-pink to match her bridesmaid's dress. Angelica has gone white to match her wedding dress and Bill and the vicar manage to catch her as she feels faint. She sits on a pew and attempts to put her head between her knees but this is not possible as there is too much wedding dress material in the way.

The church is now filled with tut-tutting. Fortunately, Angelica recovers and the marriage service continues without any further problems. The best man even makes a joke about mobiles at the reception afterwards and everyone laughs. Angelica has forgiven Becky, but Becky feels that she herself will *never* get over it.

Of course, your phone may be a lifesaver in an emergency – it is not all bad. But be thoughtful and considerate about when you use it. Also, avoid giving your parents a nasty panic attack when they receive the phone bill because you have been using the landline to phone friends on *their* mobiles. Your dad may not agree with you that you *had* to spend nearly half an hour reassuring your friend Zoë that the new red highlights in her hair really do suit her. The excuse that you had run out of credit on your mobile may not go down too well as your dad contemplates selling the family silver to meet the phone bill.

The great focal point of the entire household, of course, is not the telephone. It is not the roaring log fire, either, or even the grand piano. Nor is it the fridge. (Well, not all the time.) No, it is the TV.

• The scene - 1

Danny is staying with his step-family. He wants to watch the Belgian Grand Prix, but his step-brother and step-sisters are clamouring to watch their *Pingu* DVD for the fourth time so far that day.

• The wrong approach: Danny gets into an argument with Leonora, Theodora, Henrietta and William. Leonora, Theodora and Henrietta throw things at him, and William bursts into tears. Danny finds himself watching *Pingu* for the fourth time.

• The right approach - a simple solution:

Danny offers to take the children off his step-mother's hands for a while, for a walk to the park to feed the penguins – sorry, ducks – and play on the swings. He asks his step-mother if she will record the start of the Belgian Grand Prix for him while he is out. He can then watch it in peace later on while the children are busy having their baths.

• The scene - 2

Leonora, Theodora, Henrietta and William, not to mention Howling Henry the half-brother, are all making so much noise that Danny can hardly hear himself think. He puts on his *Skullcrusher III* DVD for them to watch, just to keep them quiet. It is extremely effective, and the children fall silent, staring at the screen. Danny settles down to enjoy some peace and quiet, until suddenly the remote control is snatched from his hand, and the TV is turned off. 'I don't think it's quite suitable, do you?' says Sienna, his step-mother.

Danny has been used to watching whatever he likes whenever he likes while he is in his own house. But at his step-mother's house, things are slightly different. This is a 'Nothing You Can Do About It' (NYCDAI) situation. This sort of situation arises quite often in every family, and it is best to accept it as part of family life.

CHAPTER 2
Family and Friends

PROBLEM 1: Going out with friends

• The scene

It is a quiet Sunday afternoon at the house of Mr and Mrs Toogood. Angelica's mum and dad are both snoring their heads off in front of a good film (black and white Second World War film) on the television. There is nothing happening. Angelica feels she might as well be dead. Suddenly the doorbell rings, and there are her friends Amy, Sam, Danny and Soumik.

'Hi, Angelica!' says Amy. 'We wondered if you'd like to come with us into town.'

The answer to this has, of course, to be YES! YES! with a fanfare of trumpets!

Then the inevitable happens. Mr and Mrs Toogood are standing there in the hall behind their daughter (why couldn't they have gone on sleeping?), *asking questions*. They ask these questions in loud, clearly audible voices, as if the friends waiting on the doorstep did not exist:

Mum: 'Who is it, dear?'
Dad: 'What do they want?'

If you find yourself in a similar situation, what sort of answer do you give?

• **Answer 1:** 'Going out now, Mum, Dad, see-youlaterrightbyeee!' and you disappear out through the door at high speed without a backward glance.

• **Answer 2:** 'It's Amy, Mum, and some friends. Hi, guys. Excuse me a moment, I've just got to get something.'

The first answer may get you out of the house quickly, but it is just storing up trouble for later, as the chances are you will find your parents still standing there sev-

eral hours later when you get back, with thunderous looks on their faces because you didn't answer their questions adequately. You may even find yourself grounded.

The second answer gives you a chance to usher your parents into another room so that you don't have an embarrassing family discussion in front of your friends. You can say encouraging things like: 'It's just the guys, Mum. Soumik's going help me with my maths. Anyway, I want to be back in time to finish my homework. So I won't be long. See you!'

As long as you don't stray too far from the truth, this kind of answer should mean you leave your parents looking faintly reassured, rather than just faint. They appreciate the fact that you took time to talk to them and that you took their natural tendency to worry into account. They will be reassured by the fact that you sound so sensible. Which you are, of course. Let's just ignore the little incident the other day when you did ten handstands in the back garden, in the hope that the boy next door, whom you fancy, would notice your legs in your skinny jeans.

Unfortunately, Angelica opted for the first answer, and disappeared out through the door at high speed.

When she returned several hours later, Mr and Mrs Toogood were waiting (there is nothing worse, or more likely to spell trouble, than a 'waiting' parent, whether it is an answer they are waiting for, a phone call, or a letter, or simply for you to return).

• The scene:

Mr Toogood: 'Come here, Angelica, we'd like a few words with you.'

Mrs Toogood: 'We've been waiting ...' (Uh oh.)

Mr Toogood: 'I think it would be nice if you told us where you were going, rather than just rush off like that.'

Mrs Toogood: 'We do worry, you know.'

Angelica: 'I know.'

Mr Toogood: 'Where have you been?'

Angelica: 'Out.'

Mr Toogood: 'We worry when you're out with that boy.'

Angelica: 'Which boy? D'you mean Sam? But you know his dad, and Sam's great – he's taking nineteen GCSEs ...' (Sorry, it's far too late for this now. Angelica's parents are in no mood to be reassured.)

Mr Toogood: 'Sam has unsuitable friends. We saw him with a group of them the other day. And wasn't that one of them tagging along with you just now? What's his name?'

Angelica: 'Oh ... er, I don't know ... Thing. I don't know his name.'

Angelica doesn't want to talk about her afternoon, and her problem is how to get her parents to drop the subject. The question uppermost in their minds now is, 'Who is Thing? And is our daughter having a thing with Thing? And will she be theeing Thing again thoon?'

They will want to know all about Thing, who his parents are, where he lives, what kind of person he is, what his intentions are, etc, etc.

The more vague Angelica is, the more suspicious they will become. It is much better to give a direct, non-vague answer to parental questions, so let's look at that scene in the Toogood house again:

Mr Toogood: 'Where have you been?'
Angelica: 'I went into town with the guys – Amy, Soumik, Danny and Sam. We didn't do very much. Just wandered around, and chatted.' (If you want to go one better than this, and really Impress a Parent, try something like, 'We went to the museum.')
Mrs Toogood: 'What's Sam's friend called? We saw him when you got back.'
Angelica: 'Matthew.' (Even if she can't really remember his name, it is much better to make one up, and she should choose a sensible, down-to-earth name.)
Mrs Toogood: 'Is he nice?'
Angelica: 'Yes. But he is very busy revising for his twenty GCSEs, and this afternoon was the only time off he's allowing himself until the exams, which are next year.'
Mr Toogood: 'What a sensible young man.'
Angelica: 'Yes. Can I go and get on with my homework now?'
Mrs Toogood: 'Of course, dear. I hope you had a nice afternoon.'

Angelica should resist the urge at this point to say, 'Not really,' because it will only lead to further questions – it is better to quit while you're ahead.

PROBLEM 2: Going to a party

• The scene

Angelica is going to Sam's party. She spends about three hours in the bathroom preparing. She has a long, hot de-stressing bath, with a few drops of lavender oil. Once out of the bath, she uses up half a can of deodorant, and then applies a cucumber and ginseng face pack. She leaves it on while she goes to style her hair. Her little sister, Becky, teases her; 'In my opinion, Jelly, you should have a total face-lift and complete body transplant. It's your only hope.'

So she shouts at Becky to 'Get lost!' and the face pack cracks and falls off. The dog runs away howling. She spends a further hour in her room creating dramatic 'hair spikes' with loads of Insanely Strong Gel. Sam should notice her now! Then she starts worrying about what to wear. She decides to go for maximum impact and wear her shortest skirt. It will be OK as long as she doesn't lean too far forward or reach up too high, or move very much. She might just sit. It is white, so she must be careful not to sit on anything which might melt. Her eyes are looking tired (from the stress of deciding what to wear), so she covers up the 'tiredness' with lots of eye-liner and mascara, which contrast quite starkly with the very pale foundation and powder with which she has chosen to cover her face and conceal the one spot which decided to appear right on the end other nose this morning. She applies half a bottle of Desire perfume,

THE WONDERS OF HAIR GEL — OR HOW TO FRIGHTEN THE MORE NERVOUS MEMBERS OF YOUR FAMILY...

FOR GOD'S SAKE, WHAT HAVE YOU DONE TO THE CAT?

and stares at herself in the mirror. The effect is truly remarkable. Sam cannot fail to notice (and smell) her now! She creeps downstairs, hoping to avoid her family altogether, and just slink out. But they are lying in wait for her ...

• What Angelica hopes her parents will say: 'Darling, you look lovely! Have a super evening!'

• **What her parents actually say:** '*You can't go out looking like that!* What sort of a party is it, anyway?'

• **What her brother says:** 'What's that awful smell?'

• **What her little sister says:** 'Sam's friends are really weird. Two of them got arrested last week.'

Angelica flies back up to her room in floods of tears and slams her bedroom door shut behind her. Mr and Mrs Toogood hear muffled shouts to the effect that she hates them all, and they 'spoil everything'.

• **What happens next:** In fact, parents don't usually want to 'spoil everything' for you. They are just worried. So Mrs Toogood will probably go up to Angelica's room and invite her to 'come out and talk'. This is probably the best thing to do.

• **Talk it over:** Angelica and her parents sit down and have a chat about important things like not having too much to drink, and being home by a certain time, and not having anything to do with the 'wrong sort'. She agrees to let her brother Grant walk her to the party, and collect her later. (In fact, Grant was invited to Sam's party, too, but he would rather stay in and watch *Star Wars*.) Angelica feels a little irritated, but at the same time it is

quite reassuring to know that her family is not too far away, should anything go wrong. She knows that Sam's parties can get a little out-of-hand (especially since his parents are away for the weekend and he is on his own in the house). It is quite possible that by midnight (or earlier) she may have had enough of the ear-drum-perforating music (Sam has rigged up speakers in every single room, even the loo, so there is no getting away from it), the flashing lights and the warm, cheap white wine. Not to mention Sam's friends.

But, in the meantime, she is all set to have a great time, so … LET'S PARTY !

But remember to be home at the right time – you have been warned!

PROBLEM 3: Bringing the boyfriend/ girlfriend home

• The scene

Soumik has spent several weeks preparing his parents for the shock of meeting his girlfriend, Natasha. It shouldn't really be a shock as Natasha is friendly, polite and very pretty, and all Soumik's mates think he is lucky. However, Soumik's parents tend to be a little wary of complete strangers, especially when their only son seems to be getting 'involved' with them. Eventually, his mother calms down, and says that Natasha must be a nice girl to be Soumik's girlfriend, and Soumik's father nods agreement. Soumik heaves a sigh of relief, and the following day he brings Natasha home after school.

• **What Soumik hopes his parents will do:** They will say something like, 'How nice to meet you, Natasha!' And then leave Soumik and Natasha to play some of their favourite music in his room.

• **What Soumik's parents actually do:** They certainly say, 'How nice to meet you, Natasha!' but there is no way they are going to leave Natasha and Soumik alone. Mrs Sen is full of questions about Natasha s family: where they live, what does her father do, how many brothers and sisters, and so on. Then she insists that Soumik and his girlfriend sit down to an enormous tea she has prepared specially for them. It is obvious by now that she likes Natasha and looks upon her as a nice friend for her son. Soumik feels awkward, but it would be a mistake to upset his mother by refusing her hospitality, and Natasha seems quite happy with the way things are going. Soumik hopes there will still be time after tea to play music to Natasha in his room. But Mrs Sen has other ideas. Straight after tea, before anyone has a chance to escape, she grabs the cherished family photo album, and shows all the photos of baby Soumik to Natasha.

'Isn't he sweet, Natasha?' she cries.

'Oh, he's just adorable!' says Natasha. Then she looks at Soumik, grins and says, 'You haven't changed much, Soumik.'

Did she *have* to say that? Soumik begins to wonder if he really wants to play music to her in his room. He feels miserable. His parents have taken over completely. Are they trying to ruin his life?

The Answer: No, of course they are not. But meeting each other for the first time can be a big shock for parents and boyfriend/girlfriend alike. They may both need a little time to come to terms with a new situation, especially if they come from different cultural backgrounds.

Here are a few suggestions for preparing your parents and your date for the shock of meeting each other:

1) It won't be such a shock if you say a little about your boyfriend/girlfriend to your parents, and vice-versa, before they actually meet. For instance:

• 'James is quite artistic.' (Translation: 'James has waist-length purple hair and wears two earrings in each ear, a nose ring and an amazing Jester's hat with bells and tassels.')

• 'Mum and Dad can't wait to meet you.' (Translation: 'Mum and Dad are sick with worry and want to see what kind of person/people I'm getting mixed up with.')

• 'Louise is a really mature person.' (Translation: 'Louise is twenty years older than me.')

• 'Josh has a great sense of humour.' (Translation: 'Josh

likes to burp loudly in public, and he does a good impression of the Teletubbies. And he owns a whoopee cushion.')

• 'Mum and Dad are really nice once you get to know them.' (Translation: 'Don't be put off if at first they stare at you as if you are an alien from the planet Zog.')

• 'Luke is amazing. He's the best – I just know you're going to love him.' (Translation: 'It doesn't really matter what I say – you still won't like him.')

• 'My parents are quite, er, you know, conventional.' (Translation: 'For God's sake don't wear your heavily ripped jeans with the flies which won't do up properly, and the black leather sleeveless shirt with loads of zips and chains, plus your cool shades and rapper hat.')

2) Once you have prepared everyone, make sure you choose a good moment to introduce them, *not* for instance, when:

i) your parents are in the middle of a blazing row.

ii) your parents have just had a blazing row and the atmosphere is frost-laden.

iii) your parents have just watched *The Ten O'Clock News* and are about to retire to bed with a mug of Horlicks.

iv) your mother is in the kitchen trying to do ten different things at once, and your father is asleep in front of the television, or vice versa.

v) the dog has just been sick, or a small sibling is having a tantrum, or the television has exploded – or all of these.
vi) your parents have just received the phone bill.

PROBLEM 4: Introducing friends to your ghastly family and emerging with your reputation intact

• The scene

Amy Average has been listening to Danny playing his saxophone at school. She thinks he is pretty cool, and he seems to like her, too. She tells him she is learning the guitar, and that all of her family are really musical.

'We just love music so much,' she says. 'My dad used to play the trumpet. I don't know if he played the saxophone as well ...'

'Really?' says Danny, sounding interested. 'I'd like to meet your dad – he sounds great. I don't see much of my own dad. He doesn't play anything.'

'Well, why don't you come and meet him?' says Amy.

'Yeah, I might just do that,' says Danny.

'After school?'

'Sure. See you later.'

• **What Amy is thinking**: 'Oh no! what have I done?' She is desperate to impress Danny because he is so cool. Now he is about to come face to face with *uncool reality* ...

• **What happens**: Amy and Danny (with his saxophone) arrive at the Average house:

'Hi, Mum. This is Danny.'

'Hello, dear,' says Mrs Average. 'Would you like to stay for tea? We're having fish and chips, Amy's favourite.'

'Er, thanks, but I'm not really hungry.'

'Kevin!' shrieks Mrs Average suddenly.

'Kevin!' shrieks the parrot, which is in a cage in the kitchen.

'My name's Danny, actually,' says Danny.

'No, Kevin is my dad's name,' Amy explains.

'Oh.'

'Where are you, Kevin?' shouts Mrs Average. 'Kevin! The kitchen sink needs unblocking!'

'Coming, dear.'

'Sorry about this,' Amy whispers to Danny. 'It's not always like this.' (Well, it is, actually.)

'Like what?' says Danny. He seems more interested in the parrot, which has put its head on one side to look at him. Danny puts his head on one side, too.

'Hi, Dad,' says Amy, as Mr Average shuffles into the kitchen wearing a favourite pair of ancient slippers. 'This is Danny.'

'Good evening, er …' says Mr Average.

'Danny,' says Danny.

'Oh … ah … that's short for Daniel, is it?'

'Yes.'

'Have a go at the sink, would you, Kevin?' says Mrs Average. 'I can't shift it. I think we need a new sink plunger.'

'Amy says you play the trumpet, Mr Average,' says Danny.

'Well, not for a long time, Danny,' replies Mr Average.

'Danny plays the saxophone,' says Amy.

'Really,' says Mr Average. 'Rather a loud instrument, isn't it?'

Mr Average turns his attention to the blocked sink, and Danny talks to the parrot. The next member of the Average family to arrive on the scene is Gran. Gran is about ninety years old and very deaf, and inclined to tell the parrot to 'Speak up!'

'Hello, Donny!' she says. 'I've heard a lot about you!'

'His name's Danny, Gran!' shouts Amy.

'Donny!' insists Gran, who doesn't like being argued

with. 'I knew a young American serviceman once. His name was Donny. He was a one for the ladies! You'll be a one for the ladies, too, in a couple of years' time, no doubt!' says Gran to Danny, tweaking him on the cheek.

'Er, Gran!' says Amy, hugely embarrassed.

'What's for supper, Mum?' asks Amy's little brother, Alex, running into the kitchen and stopping to stare hard at Danny. 'Are you Amy's boyfriend?' Snigger, snigger. 'Cor! Is that a saxophone? Can you play it? Oh, please!'

Danny plays a few notes to the accompaniment of Mr Average on the sink plunger, unblocking the sink. Suddenly there is an enormous gurgle. 'There, that's done it!' says Mr Average. 'It's all going down the drain now.'

It certainly is, thinks Amy. It seems as though any hope she ever had of getting a good thing going with Danny has just gone down the drain, along with her reputation. Her family are *awful*. She will never live it down.

Here are a few tactics for preserving your own reputation as far as possible:

1) Choose a time when you know the more embarrassing members of your family are likely to be out, so you can introduce your friends to the ones who are less embarrassing.

2) Explain to your friends afterwards that your father has been under a lot of strain recently, which is why he is wearing his pullover tucked into a pair of baggy stonewashed jeans, and 'dancing' to your music while he redecorates the living-room.

3) You can always blame your parents' more embarrassing behaviour on the fact that they had 'a difficult upbringing', or are suffering from 'executive stress'.

4) If your mother has a tendency to put her arm around you in front of your friends, twiddle your hair and say things like, 'So how's Mummy's little sausage today, then?', it is best to answer, 'Fine,' and quickly change the subject by saying something like, 'Have you seen my shades anywhere. Mum?'

5) Bribe little sisters and little brothers to leave you alone. Tell them you will let them play your latest computer game later (they are already better at it than you are) if they will disappear or simply keep their mouths shut while your friends are around.

6) Focus on your family's best points, such as your father's sports trophies (he was runner up in the All-Essex Badminton Finals twenty years ago), a series of brilliant watercolours of flowers your mother once did, which are now framed and on the wall (directing your friends' attention at something like this means they hopefully won't see your sister appear briefly in the doorway wearing a floral shower-cap, her face coated in a home-made egg and cress face pack). Or simply

focus on a delicious cake your mother has just made, which will distract attention from the fact that your father is now wearing a frilly white apron over his stonewashed jeans while he stuffs dried apricots, prunes and garlic up a chicken for tonight's supper (his own recipe). If all else fails, the family can provide a welcome distraction.

OH, HE'S JUST SOOO CUTE!

7) Check out your room before you take your friends up there in case your mother has been in there tidying, and has done things like lay your Barbie pyjamas (several sizes too small but you still wear them) out on your bed, neatly folded. Or if she has put a pile of clothes from the airing-cupboard on your bed, and on the top, clearly visible, a pair of Winnie the Pooh knickers.

PROBLEM 5: When your parents don't like your friends

• The scene – 1

Angelica brings Sam home for the first (and last?) time to meet her family.

'Mum, Dad. This is Sam. Sam, these are my parents.'

'Er, it's great to meet you, Mr and Mrs Toobad, er, oh God, I mean, Toogood, sorry, I, er …'

'So, you're Sam.'

'Yes. Sir.'

There follows a long silence during which all members of the family stop whatever they're doing and stare at Sam as though he is an alien from another planet. Only Horace the dog is friendly, gets up and wanders across the room, wagging his tail, to sniff at Sam's jeans.

'We've heard a lot about you, Sam,' says Mrs Toogood, rather worryingly. (What have they heard?)

'And all of it's true!' says Sam, attempting a joke to lighten the atmosphere. This doesn't work.

'Is it true you pulled your trousers down and mooned at a policeman?' asks Becky. 'And were you arrested?'

Angelica hisses at her to, 'Shut up!'

'Er, me and Sam are going up to my room to chat,' says Angelica.

The expression on Mr Toogood's face says it all. He will have *words* with his elder daughter later on.

• What Angelica hopes her father will say later on: 'Sam seems like a nice young man. You must invite him round here more often.'

• What Mr Toogood will actually say: 'Don't ever ever bring that ... that Thing here again! And you are not to go to his house, either.'

• The Conclusion: Angelica concludes that it was not such a good idea to bring Sam home. Some things will never work. Sometimes, trying to introduce your boyfriend/girlfriend to your family is like trying to mix oil and water. It is doomed from the start. But there are tactics you can try in order to soften the blow:

1) Take the boyfriend/girlfriend into the kitchen, rather than straight up to your bedroom (even if you really are only going to chat). This will make your parents feel more involved and will stop their imaginations running riot.

2) You can't expect your parents to like your friends if the friends show no respect, basic courtesy, etc, or don't even so much as acknowledge your parents' existence, apart from a slight nod of the head, or semi-audible grunt. Don't be afraid to tell your friends to obey certain house rules, such as not helping themselves straight from the fridge, not putting their feet on the furniture and not snogging on the sofa.

3) Your parents are less likely to welcome your friends if they feel that their house has been invaded and taken over, even to the extent, for instance, of finding the bathroom occupied by two friends busy bleaching their hair. You must leave your parents with somewhere to escape to on their own, if they want to.

4) Say to your parent, some time after the friend they don't like has left, 'Hey, Mum/Dad, Sam (or whoever) really liked you. He said he thought I was lucky to have such great parents.' Of course, Sam has probably said no such thing, but it will make your parents stop and think a bit – maybe there is some good in him, after all. They may be more prepared to give him a chance, next time. And if he blows that, of course – well, is he really your type, anyway?

5) If your parents are judging your friend merely by their appearance (they don't go for the friend's purple Mohican haircut in a big way), then it is probably just a matter of time before they realise that the friend has redeeming qualities. Point out to your parents gently that whoever it is simply would not be a friend of yours if they were not intelligent, sensitive, kind, generous and caring, with a good sense of humour. It is quite difficult for a parent to argue with this.

• The scene – 2

It is like a scene from *Romeo and Juliet*. Sam is climbing up the wall to Angelica's bedroom, since Mr and Mrs Toogood won't let him in through the front door. He holds on to the tree which Mr Toogood has been training to grow against the wall for several years, and he climbs up it nearly to the top, which is just below Angelica's windowsill. Unfortunately, the tree comes

away from the wall, Sam loses his grip and falls sideways on to the rubbish bins below, disturbing a couple of lovesick cats, who let out a tremendous yowl, and there is a crash and clang and clatter of bins and tins, and rubbish everywhere.

Angelica is really fed up. She has been to a lot of trouble getting herself ready for Sam.

Sam tries again. This time he brings a ladder, and leans it up against Angelica's windowsill. He nearly makes it into her bedroom, until he realises that Mr and Mrs Toogood are in there with her, sitting on the bed and trying to talk some sense into her (waste of time). Needless to say, Sam doesn't hang around, or rather he does, as his shirt gets hooked up on the ladder, but what happens to him after this no one knows, as Mrs Toogood slams down the window and draws the curtains.

Mr Toogood over-reacts a bit by installing barbed wire and an electric fence all round the house. Mrs Toogood tells him that he is 'going to have to let Angelica go' sooner or later. Let her go? Becky comments that she would have given her away years ago.

• The moral of this tale: Don't behave like Romeo and Juliet. You know what happened to them.

• The right thing to do: Don't try to go behind your parents' backs. You will only succeed in putting their backs up. It is better to sit down and have a chat with them. Mention that everyone has *some* good points, and that the boy they don't approve of, for instance, has offered to redecorate your bedroom for you. Would they allow him to do it, on condition that the door was kept open at all times (the room needs to be well-ventilated)? Find an excuse for your parents to get to know whoever it is they don't like, and they will probably find out he or she isn't as bad as they thought. (If he or she is as bad as your parents thought, or maybe worse, then give up.)

PROBLEM 6: Having a party

• The scene
Amy wants to throw a party, and she wants it to be cool.

• What Amy hopes her parents will say:
'Yes, of course you can have a party. We'll go out that evening, so you can have the house to yourselves.'

• What Amy's parents actually say: 'Oh no,
not a party! When do you want it? Saturday? We'd better not go to the committee meeting that night, Kevin. We'll have to stay here and keep an eye on them all. OK, dear, you can have a party, on condition we vet all the guests.'

• How many guests?
Which of the following questions is more likely to succeed?

i) 'Mum, can I have a party for fifty-seven people?'
ii) 'Mum, can I have a few friends round for a party?'

The correct answer is, of course, number (ii). Once you have got your parents' consent, and issued the invitations (verbal/written/scented/embossed, or whatever), you can always ask, 'Mum, is it all right if a few of my friends bring a few of their friends?' And, later on, 'Mum, is it all right if some of my friends' friends bring a few of *their* friends. They're worried they won't know anyone if they don't bring some people they already know.' Your parent may make a half-hearted effort to grapple with the logic of this statement, but the effort is futile since it is far too late now, the party is GO.

Then there are the preparations. The Average family moves the furniture around a bit, but there doesn't really seem to be any more space for dancing than there was before.

'How about food?' says Mrs Average.

'And I suppose you'll want something to drink,' says Mr Average.

• **What Amy hopes her parents will say next:** 'I'll make an enormous bowl of chilli, and some avocado and cream cheese dips, with lots of crisps and things.' (Mrs Average) 'Oh, and garlic bread.'

'I'll get six cases of white wine, and six of red. Will that be enough, do you think?' (Mr Average)

• **What Amy's parents actually say**: 'You'd better help me make the sandwiches, Amy. I can do ham, Philadelphia cheese, or Marmite. And sausages on sticks. And do your friends like jelly?'

'Mum!' moans Amy. 'It's not, like, a children's party, you know. I'm nearly fifteen.'

'Sorry, Amy. I know, I'll make you something special!'

Amy's eyes light up.

'Yes,' continues Mrs Average. 'A trifle!'

Mr Average, meanwhile, is offering to make a large bowl of party punch. 'It'll be mostly lemonade, of course,' he says. 'But I'll put in one bottle of wine if you like. We've still got some of that non-alcoholic English wine left, haven't we, dear? That'll do. Now – what are we going to do about music?'

• **What Amy hopes her parents will say**:
'We'll hire a DJ for the night.'

• **What Amy's parents actually say**: You can use the hi-fi, Amy, but not too loud. I think your father's still got some music suitable for young people's parties, haven't you, Kevin?'

What can Amy do to avert total disaster? Should she cancel the party completely? But it's too late. She's invited everyone. The best thing to do is accept her parents' well-meant offers of help, and realise that this is a NYCDAI (Nothing You Can Do About It) situation, except make the best of it.

THE PARTY

Everyone is in party mood, especially Mr and Mrs Average, who are dancing what looks like the twist in the middle of the floor while the teenage guests stand around the edge of the room watching them with a mixture of amusement and embarrassment. Danny arrives with his mother.

'I couldn't stop her,' he mutters to Amy. 'She loves going to parties.'

Mrs Broke has brought a bottle of wine, and she drinks most of it. She then dances a jitterbug with Mr Average in the middle of the room while the teenage guests watch, fascinated.

Amy notices that Danny has disappeared. She finds him sitting alone in a room upstairs, reading. 'Are you all right?' she asks.

'It's Mum,' he replies, quietly. This seems to explain everything.

So what do you do if your family embarrasses you at your own party? You can either do what Danny did, and retire quietly from the scene, and read a book. Or, alternatively, you can have several glasses of party punch – and join in the fun! Show the old folks some real dancing! Put on some real music. In fact, this is probably the best answer of all. Because as soon as you put on Dr Drear and the Deadheads at full volume there will be a mass exodus of everyone over the age of twenty-five from the room. They will all escape to the kitchen and close the door in an effort to shut out the noise. And

you and your friends will be left on your own to enjoy yourselves.

What do you do if your parents refuse to make themselves scarce?

Answer: Go and have the party in your room. It may be a little cramped, but it is a good excuse to get close to someone you like. If you are a girl, your parents will probably let the girls sleep over. The boys will be thrown out at some point.

Finally, here is a four-point Party Plan:

1) Make a guest list. This is loads of fun, especially if you draw up the list in the company of some friends. You can decide who you want to ask, and why, and who you don't want to ask, and why. When you've got it all worked out, put it away in a secret place. Now draw up another list, this time of people you know you can safely invite into your house without your father having a fit, and your mother putting her foot down and saying, 'Never again!' to any more parties.

2) Bribe any small brothers or sisters to stay in their rooms, by offering them endless turns at your latest

OH – AREN'T THEY CUTE?

computer game if they promise not to appear so much as once in their Spider-Man pyjamas, giggling and demanding drinks, and being as silly as they possibly can (that's *very silly*). Add a little blackmail if you like, warning them that you will tell Mum who trimmed the cat's and the hamster's whiskers, if they dare to appear.

3) Make sure that any embarrassing photos of yourself taken several years ago, grinning like a complete idiot in your school uniform, are safely put away before the guests arrive.

ER — THAT'S NOT ME... ER — I DON'T KNOW WHO THAT IS...

4) If it is summer, have a barbecue. Hang up lanterns and fairy lights, and see your rather unexciting patch of grass and assorted shrubs transformed into a magical enchanted place. With any luck, your parents will soon find it a 'little chilly' and retire indoors to watch *The Ten O'Clock*

News, leaving you and your friends to dance in the dark. Or if it is really hot, suggest a water fight. This will give you a good excuse to get the person you fancy really wet so that they have to take their clothes off.

And remember: if you ever want to have another party, make sure you help clear up afterwards.

PROBLEM 7: Little friends

• The scene

Amy Average's little brother's little friends are driving her mad. They keep charging around the house making screeching noises and loud war-cries while she is trying to concentrate on a magazine. 'Shut it, Pest!' she shouts at Alex. He takes no notice. She throws her magazine at him, and retreats to her bedroom and closes the door. She

can hear Pest and his friends giggling just outside. They are obviously plotting something.

• **The wrong approach** to this sort of Persistent Family Pest Syndrome Number Two is to shout at your little brother and his friends, and let them know that they are getting to you. This will only make them worse.

• **The right approach** is to appear totally cool and unbothered by anything they do. They will soon lose interest. This is the case with any kind of teasing, either within the family or from outside.

Amy also remembers that one of her brother's friends is the younger brother of a boy she fancies at school. This might be a way of getting to know more about him!

CHAPTER 3
Family and School

PROBLEM 1: Not wanting to go

• The scene

The alarm goes off, the parrot starts shrieking, Mrs Average hammers on her daughter's door. 'Time to get up, Amy!' Amy groans and pulls a pillow over her head. She doesn't want to get up − ever. She is suffering from Total Not Wanting To Go To School Syndrome, for which there are several reasons you can give your parents:

Amy: 'I just want to sleep. Go away and let me sleep. I didn't get to bed until one a.m.'
Mrs Average: 'Go to bed earlier.'
Amy: 'Everybody hates me and I don't have any friends.'
Mrs Average: 'I'm sure that's not true. We could have a chat with your teacher, if you're really worried.'
Amy: 'I hate school, and I'm not going.'
Mrs Average: 'Oh yes, you are.'
Amy: 'Oh no, I'm not. Oh, Mum, please don't send me! It's awful!'
Mrs Average: 'Well, we'd better see your headmaster, and get this sorted out.' (This may be a good first step in the right direction. If you are being bullied, for instance, you should bring the problem to as many people's attention as

I AM UNWELL

possible, so that the problem can be *stopped*.)

Amy: 'I have Severe Allergy to School Syndrome.' (S.A.T.S.S.)

Mrs Average: 'What's that? Perhaps we'd better see the doctor/school psychologist.' *(This tactic will at least get you off school for a few hours.)*

Amy: 'I haven't done my homework.'

Mrs Average: 'Make sure you do it next time.'

Amy: 'I have no hope of passing my exams.'

Mrs Average: 'Then get to school as quickly as possible so the teachers can help you pass them.'

Amy: 'I am unwell.'

Mrs Average: 'Here are some paracetamol – you'd better hurry or you'll be late for school.'

Amy: 'I'm so popular. The boys all want to go out with me. I need some time and space on my own.'
Mrs Average: 'So do I. Now go to school.'

In short: unless you're really unwell, you'll just have to lump it until you leave school.

PROBLEM 2: Homework

Why not turn homework to your advantage, and get it sorted at the same time? The Homework Excuse is the best excuse for getting out of difficult situations and things you would rather not do.

HAVE YOU DONE YOUR HOMEWORK?

• The scene

Soumik's Aunt Sita and her son and daughter have come to tea. Soumik's mother has produced the cherished family album of photographs of baby Soumik with no clothes on, and his cousins are helpless with mirth, all at Soumik's expense. As the final straw, Soumik's mother suddenly says: 'By the way, it is about time you should know – my baby Soumik has a girlfriend! She is a very nice girl, and of course she is also very lucky to be the girlfriend of my Soumik. Her name is Natasha ...'

Soumik's cousins and his Aunt Sita are all staring at him in a way which makes Soumik wonder whether his flies are undone. There is only one thing to say, in a situation like this: 'Er, I've got an awful lot of homework to do – I really must go and get on with it, if you don't mind.' And he disappears at high speed through the door, and locks himself in his room.

Here are some thoughts on how to handle homework (read carefully and then write a six-page essay on why homework is a good idea, and also why it isn't):

1) It is a good idea to get your homework sorted, rather than let it all pile up (literally) and get on top of you. Try to make it as enjoyable as possible:

i) You could go to a friend's house to work. Tell your parent you are working on a project together, or you need your friend's help with something. This will give you a chance to do your homework (of course) *and* catch up on some gossip.

ii) Tell your parent you can only work in your room with The Gobsmackers' latest album playing at full volume (even through headphones this tends to make ornaments on shelves shake and rattle). If this, or something similar, happens to be true, there is not a lot anyone (or any parent) can do about it – except let you get on with it.

iii) A bag of Beastly Crunch, a can of Ting, or even a tube of Smarties may help you to concentrate.

2) When it comes to homework, there are two kinds of parent:

i) Parents who love to help you with your homework because it gives them the chance to show how frightfully clever they are, and how, basically, they know everything.

ii) Parents who hate being asked to help you with your homework because, er, basically they know nothing, and were perfect dunces at school.

There is one thing which every parent will say at one time or another: 'Go and get on with your homework!'

There are two reasons why a parent will say this:

i) They want you to do well at school, pass all your GCSEs, win a scholarship to Oxford and become the next Prime Minister.

ii) They want you out of the way because they are trying to have a serious talk with your mother/father/chat with a friend/get on with some work of their own/watch their favourite TV programme in peace.

Whatever their motive for urging you to get on with it, there is only one person who can *make* you do your homework – and that is you. It is much better, really, to get it out of the way. Then you can go and watch your favourite DVD with a clear conscience. And, who knows, you may win a scholarship to Oxford and become the next Prime Minister (God forbid).

PROBLEM 3: School reports

• The scene – 1

Angelica has brought home her school report. Here is part of it:

History: Angelica's essay on Roman Britain was excellent. Unfortunately, we were studying the Tudors at the time. Angelica needs to concentrate so that she knows which books to read, and what period of history the rest of the class is studying. D

French: Angelica has a very limited French vocabulary, consisting of the words 'Oui', 'Non', 'Bonjour' and 'Au revoir'. D

Art and Ceramics: Angelica has difficulty with pencil control, paintbrush control, control of clay and any kind of control, including self-control. D

Craft, Design and Technology: Angelica makes interesting things out of old cereal packets and cardboard tubes. However, at the age of fifteen I cannot help feeling that she should be moving on from this sort of thing. C

These are her best subjects and her best marks. The rest of the report is worse, and it ends with the headmaster's comment, as follows:

'I would like to see a marked improvement in Angelica's behaviour. I was disappointed to hear that she was late for school every morning throughout the term.'

This is a seriously bad report. Angelica hides in her room and waits for the inevitable: 'Angelica! We'd like a word with you!'

• **What Angelica hopes her parents will say:** 'This is not a good report, but it could be worse. We understand you've been under a lot of pressure, and you mustn't get too stressed. We're on your side, you know. Your father and I will sort everything out. Don't worry, Angel. Good results aren't everything.'

• What Angelica's parents actually say:

'This report could not be worse. What have you got to say for yourself?'

What can Angelica possibly say to calm her parents down? She could try something like: 'I know I haven't done very well. Mum and Dad, but now I have a chance to learn from my mistakes, and do better. With your continuing love, support and encouragement, I can do this. I love you. You're the best.' She gives her mother a big hug. Then she gives her father a big hug. It is much more difficult for parents to be angry after a scene like this.

• The scene – 2

Soumik has brought home a very good report. Here is part of it:

Maths: Brilliant. Superb. A joy to teach. A*

English: Wonderful, wonderful essays. What a star! I'm totally gobsmacked! A*

Physical Education: An Olympic gold medal-winner in the making. This boy should go far, especially in the long-jump. A*****

Music: Soumik is extremely talented. A**

The headmaster's comment:

'We are fortunate indeed to have your son at St Herbert's. Well done, Soumik!'

_____

Soumik's parents are beaming with pride and admiration for their son. Soumik chooses this moment to ask if they would consider getting him the bass guitar he has always wanted.

• What Soumik's parents say: 'Of course! Whatever our brilliant Soumik wants, he shall have!'

In other words, if you should be fortunate enough/ outstandingly clever enough to get a really good school report, this is the ideal time to ask your parent for something you have always wanted. They are much more likely to say yes.

PROBLEM 4: Younger siblings spilling your uncool secrets

• The scene

Becky and her friends, Jo, Jess and Jenny, are all clustered together in a corner of the playground, giggling. Whenever Angelica goes anywhere near, they burst out laughing. Angelica gets suspicious.

'What's the matter with you guys?' she asks.

'Nothing,' replies Becky. 'Why don't you go and look at the school noticeboard?'

With a sinking feeling, Angelica turns and heads for the entrance to the school, where the noticeboard is. As she walks away, Becky's friends call out after her, in loud voices, just as Sam and his friends wander past.

Jo: 'Is it true you still suck your thumb when you're going to sleep?'

Jess: 'Is it true you cuddle a stuffed pink elephant called Eric when you're in bed?'

Jenny: 'And is it true Eric's really smelly because you won't let anyone wash him?'

HA HA HA. Their hoots of merriment follow her into the school, where she finds, pinned to the noticeboard, an exercise book in which she writes poems about her feelings and all sorts of things. It is open at the page on which she has written a poem called *Longing*:

LONGING

I long for you
I long to feel your arms
Around me.
I am longing, longing, longing.
But you are a long, long way away
Even though you are quite close.
I long to tell you how I feel.
But I am afraid. I am not always strong.
But I long to belong
To you.

Underneath the poem, she has written; *I dedicate this poem, and my heart, my body and my mind to Sam Cash, my inspiration.*

'Great poem, kid,' says a voice over her shoulder. It is Sam. Her life is over. She just wants to *die*. More than that, she wants Becky to die. She is going to *murder* her. Twice.

If you find yourself in this sort of situation, and you have just been hit by twenty thousand megavolts of sheer embarrassment, and it is all the fault of your horrid little brother/sister, there are a few things you should remember:

1) Affectionate teasing taken too far can be hurtful and/or embarrassing, but your brother or sister may not have meant to cause you hurt or embarrassment. They will probably be sorry when they find out how upset you are (yes, they definitely *will* be sorry).

2) Before you panic that everyone will be laughing at you for ever and ever, remember that you are far more worried about it (whatever it is) than anyone else is likely to be. Other people are far more likely to be concerned about things relating to themselves. They couldn't care less if you went to bed with twenty stuffed and smelly pink elephants.

3) People who get a kick out of seizing on your weak points and laughing their heads off aren't worth bothering with, anyway. They are probably deeply insecure types who have to pick on others in order to bolster their own egos. Try imagining them in the most uncool situation you can (on the loo, for instance), and don't let them get to you.

4) The nicer people (who *are* worth bothering with) will probably be amused by the uncool secrets your siblings have spilled, but their amusement will be mixed with a kind of sympathetic fellow feeling because they too have many an uncool secret, which they may now feel encouraged to disclose. This could lead to a more open and honest relationship, and a lot of laughs, too. You could even end up thanking your dear little brother/sister for revealing to the world the fact that you are *human*.

5) But if you'd rather your sibling shuts up from now on, try a little gentle retaliation. For instance, why not stand up in front of the whole school during morning assembly, and announce: 'Did you know that my brother Alex has a fluffy pink teddy called Teddy-Poo whom he talks to in bed at night? And I really think you ought to know that today he is wearing his underpants back to front. He's used to Mum helping him to get dressed, you see.'

This sort of approach may guarantee that your brother/sister gives you no more grief for quite a long time (they are totally terrified of you), but you may have to explain to your parents why little Alex/Amelia-Jane is too deeply traumatised to go to school, and requires counselling by a trained professional.

6) On the whole, it is better to be kind and rise above it all, or show that it really doesn't bother you what they say. In fact, nothing they can do or say gets to you or winds you up for the simple reason that you really are super-cool and totally together. They will then find it's no fun even trying to embarrass you, and will leave you alone.

7) And one further thought – if you upset them at home, they are more likely to get their own back at school. However, if you are a really terrific older brother/sister, always kind, generous, lending them your clothes, music, books, computer games, etc and a real tower of strength when they need you – in other words, their *friend* – they are not going to behave like horrid little beasts, are they? (Well, not *all* the time, anyway.) Get them on your side. There is strength in numbers. So, whether you have one, two or even eight little brothers and sisters at your school, make sure you turn this to your advantage. You want them to look up to you (even if they are already taller than you).

PROBLEM 5: Older siblings (Why can't you be more like your wonderful sister/brother?)

Now let's suppose that the trainer is on the other foot, so to speak. You are the little sister/brother doing your best to embarrass your big sister/brother at school. Why are you doing it? 'Because I hate their guts,' is not really an adequate answer. We have to look a little further and maybe discover why you hate their guts (or think you do).

• The scene

Grant Toogood has just brought home the most startlingly brilliant school report ever written, since the very dawn of school reports, when the first ever teacher etched the first ever report on a tablet of stone, to be carried home with considerable difficulty by the first ever pupil. In other words, it is a seriously excellent report. Grant has got straight As in all subjects, and in all his exams, including a new category of result invented specially for him, a Totally Super Duper A**★★★** for Exceptional Ability in All Areas. He has now officially left school, but is going back on Speech Day to collect most of the prizes, give a speech thanking his teachers and the headmaster, and have the new Science Wing named after him (Mr and Mrs Toogood have given a donation to show their gratitude, and also because Angelica accidentally blew up the old Science Wing).

HURRAH!
SPEECH!
HURRAH!

• What Mr and Mrs Toogood are likely to say to Angelica, at frequent intervals: 'Why can't you be more like Grant?'

This is a difficult question to answer.

• Obvious answer: 'Because I'm not Grant. I'm *me*.'

• **Bad answer:** 'Because Grant is a horrid swot, goody-goody and complete nerd, and I wouldn't want to be like him if you paid me.'

• **Good answer:** 'I admire Grant very much. I think it would help me to be more like him if I could have his room now that he is off to university. Then I can read all his wonderful books, and use his computer to help me with my studies. I am of the opinion that an increase in my allowance would enable me to travel into town on a more frequent basis, and visit museums and libraries more often, like Grant does. I could also visit bookshops and add to my own collection of improving literature and general reference books.' And so on.

If you are unconvinced that this sort of subtle persuasion would work, here are some Alternative Approaches:

1) Try stealing your sibling's thunder. Get an even better school report than theirs, if it kills you (and it probably will). If this is just not possible, show your parents that you have other equally admirable qualities, such as a flair for tidying the whole house, a willingness to walk the dog, feed the cat, clean out the rabbit hutch, etc, or simply a cheerful and pleasant manner, so that they really enjoy having you around. Locking yourself in your room, sulking, glaring and giving looks that could kill at three hundred yards, will do nothing to help your case.

2) Find your sibling's Achilles' Heel. This is nothing to do with Athlete's Foot. It simply means finding the one thing they are not good at, or the one thing they have either failed or forgotten to do. Gently remind them, in front of your parents: 'Oh, Grant, I noticed the expensive new shirt that Mum bought you recently is stuffed under your bed and hasn't been washed for three weeks. I also noticed it's been badly torn. Would you like me to wash

" ..A REALLY MATURE, THOUGHTFUL AND CONSIDERATE PERSON... A SHINING EXAMPLE FOR EVERYONE TO FOLLOW "

and iron it for you? And I'll mend the hole, if you like. Oh, of course, Mum, it'll be no trouble. It's a real pleasure to help you. You have enough to do, looking after all of us, especially Grant – we all know he's too busy studying to do much to help round here. But never mind. You've always got me. You only have to ask.' Creep, creep.

PROBLEM 6: Ambitious parents

What do you do if you have ambitious parents? They are very hard to please, because they have set their hearts on you succeeding at all the things they consider important, regardless of how clever you are (or aren't). They have a kind of fixed idea in their minds that you are totally brilliant, so when you fail elementary needlework (how to thread a needle in under three hours), they will look around for someone to blame. And they are more likely to blame your school, and falling standards nationwide, rather than admit the possibility that their child prodigy (you) is not quite as brilliant as they thought and is, er, how shall we put it, 'university challenged'.

The really sad thing about all this is that the more your parents expect of you, the more likely they are to be disappointed, and that is certainly not fair on you. The important thing is somehow to make these ambitious parents look in a new direction, and actually to get to know *you*, as you are, with all sorts of good qualities and hidden talents and abilities which have so far been neglected or overlooked. For instance, they may want you to become 'something big in the city' (and they don't mean drive a double-decker bus), but the fact is that you are lousy at maths and don't understand money. How do you make them understand that all you want to do is work with animals? This is where your school, if it is a good school, could actually be quite useful, in bringing the true facts to your parents' attention. This may be a difficult or even painful process, but the fact is that both your parents and your school should want the best for you and they usually do, and it is just a matter of finding out what this is. The best person to ask, of course, is you.

• The scene

Sam Cash is having breakfast with his parents (black coffee and toast) before they go off to work, and he goes off to school. There is a lot of conversation going on, but none of it involves Sam. Both parents are talking on their mobiles to their business partners, while eating toast. Sam is wearing his cool shades, as usual. He has also bleached his hair (he looks like a mad haystack) and has taken to wearing a series of increasingly extraordinary hats, in the hope that his parents might actually notice him. But they never do.

His mother gets a letter. It is from the school. The headmaster of St Herbert's is concerned because Sam is falling so far behind that he sometimes doesn't even make it to school at all.

'Falling behind?' exclaims his mother. 'But surely you must be well ahead of everyone. I mean, let's face it, you'll be joining your father's business, or mine, in a few years' time – or even starting one of your own!'

'I blame the school,' says Mr Cash. 'They're obviously failing our son. We'd better go and see them.'

The scene changes to the headmaster's office at St Herbert's. Mrs Cash is wearing her super-smart executive trouser suit, and carries a briefcase. She looks like some-

one out of an American soap opera (perfect hair, teeth, make-up, etc). Mr Cash looks harrassed, and he carries his mobile and laptop. Sam is wearing a pair of old grey school trousers, sawn off at the knee to make a trendy pair of shorts, a white (sort of) shirt with all the buttons undone and a school tie tied around his head, bandanna-style. He is also wearing one of his hats and his cool shades. Everyone waits while Mr Cash checks his Inbox and Mrs Cash takes a call on her mobile. Finally, every-one is ready to talk about Sam.

'I am a little worried about Sam,' confesses the head-master (whose name is Trusscott).

'Perhaps you should be more worried about your teaching methods,' replies Mr Cash, challengingly.

'They're obviously failing our son. The teachers them-selves, perhaps, should share the blame?'

'I'm not seeking to blame anyone,' says Mr Trusscott, patiently. 'We have some excellent teachers at St Herbert's, and I assure you that every effort has been made to help Sam.'

'But it's just not good enough,' says Mrs Cash. 'In a few years' time, Sam will be running his own business.'

Mr Trusscott looks quite alarmed at the prospect. 'I'm not sure if that's a very good idea,' he suggests, tenta-tively. 'Sam has difficulty with numbers above ten, and he was bottom of the class in computer studies. He wrote a short essay about *Tomb Raider* for his exam, and then fell asleep.'

Now it is Mr and Mrs Cash's turn to look startled. 'But Sam has a natural flair for communication,' says Mrs Cash, 'which is important when you're running a busi-ness.'

'I'm not sure his teachers would agree,' replies Mr Trusscott. 'We all have a certain amount of difficulty understanding what he says. He does tend to mumble. The head of English Studies thought he was talking a dif-ferent language.'

'Oh.' Mr and Mrs Cash look thoroughly crestfallen.

'However,' says Mr Trusscott. 'We are all very pleased with Sam's progress in woodwork. He has a real talent. We first noticed his natural ability when he carved his initials all over a desk, and also on the door to the boys' lavatory. So we harnessed his obvious creative energy, and allowed him to apply it freely in woodwork. Sam has now made a number of shelves, an intricately-carved box for which he is to be awarded the School Art Prize, and I understand he is currently working on a small table.'

'I knew it!' cries Mrs Cash triumphantly. 'He can start his own furniture business, like the queen's nephew. He'll make a fortune!' She gives Sam a hug (something she hasn't done for a very long time), and knocks his hat sideways.

Let's face it – some parents will never learn.

So what can you do if your parents' ambitions outweigh your ability?

1) Tell them you're worried about letting them down. Most parents will be completely horrified that you should feel like this, and they will go out of their way to reassure you that you have their love and support, no matter what, and they will probably step back a bit and re-examine the whole situation. This should lead to a new understanding.

2) If they have set their hearts on you becoming a real Whizz Kid on the Stock Exchange, or a Captain of Industry or something else that sounds equally unlikely, while you have decided that your future lies in the local supermarket, stacking shelves, have a chat about it. If they are aiming too high, it is also possible that you are aiming too low. You should be able to work out a middle course that sounds more reasonable, and should suit everyone, especially you.

PROBLEM 7: When your parents come to school

• The scene

Mr and Mrs Toogood have just arrived at St Herbert's Open Day. Angelica is already at the school, practising with the choir, who are going to sing to the parents in the school playground, as it is a nice day. The choir is in the middle of practising one of the quieter songs.

'Darling!' shouts Mrs Toogood. 'Angel! Yoo hoo! Here we are!' She waves wildly, as if she hasn't seen Angelica for months, and the whole choir, teachers and other parents turn to look.

Mrs Toogood has really gone to town and dressed up for the occasion. She is wearing a brilliant emerald-green skirt, an electric-blue jacket with a fluffy collar and cuffs, and several layers of eyeliner and pink lipstick. Unfortunately, one of her dark tan stockings is badly laddered, but she is wearing her white high-heeled shoes, which are also her noisiest shoes, specially designed to clatter loudly on polished floorboards, such as they have at St Herbert's.

Mr Toogood is wearing a baggy navy suit and a wide red tie, and a new pair of black leather shoes which creak loudly with every footstep.

Later on, taking her parents around the school, it seems to Angelica that everyone turns to see what the clack, clack, creak, creak noise is, as her parents parade through St Herbert's in their smart shoes. But did they have to wear such very LOUD shoes? Did her mother

have to wear such LOUD clothes? Did her father have to wear such a LOUD tie? Do they have to talk in such LOUD voices? Are they deliberately trying to draw attention to themselves? Yes, of course they are. They are enjoying themselves. They are extremely proud of their daughter, and of her part in the life of the school, and they want everyone to know that they are there for her. She, on the other hand, wishes they weren't.

Here are some of the embarrassing things your parents may do at Open Day, or on Sports Day, or almost any day in fact, and some suggestions for handling a potentially problematic Parent-in-Public situation:

1) Your mother is calling out to you in a very loud voice, 'Darling! It's me! Here I am!' (Yes, you know who she is, and you know she's there. So does the whole of the rest of the school.) What do you do if everyone is looking at her, and at you?

i) Don't let embarrassment override every other feeling. Perhaps your mother is quite attractive, or has a sparkling, extrovert personality. So perhaps the looks she's attracting are admiring ones.

ii) On the other hand, if your mother looks like a giant ice-cream sundae on legs, and there is simply no hope for her (or for you, just at that precise moment), you could try saying something along the lines of: 'Mum has a sister who's deaf, and she's so used to speaking in a loud voice to her that she doesn't realise she's speaking like that all the time,' and, 'Mum has another sister who's partially-sighted so she has to dress in bright colours so her sister can see her.' Your friends will then realise that your mother has a lot to cope with, so it's not surprising if she looks a bit strange.

2) Parents also find it hard to resist making comments about your friends:

'Oh look, dear, there's that boy Amy's always talking about! It's Nathan, isn't it, dear? He's your boyfriend, isn't he? He looks nice, doesn't he? His parents look nice, too. Shall we go and say hello?'

This is, of course, horribly embarrassing for you. You fancy Nathan like anything, but you would *die* if he knew. And the last thing in the world you want to do is introduce your dreadful parents. So what do you do?

i) Turn and flee at high speed and hide in the school

broom cupboard. This doesn't really achieve anything, unless you find that Nathan has already had the same idea (he saw your mother approaching) and is hiding in the broom cupboard, too.

ii) Alternatively, if you can bear to look in his direction, you might notice that Nathan is looking at you, rather strangely (but not unpleasantly). Perhaps he has overheard what your mother said, and hadn't realised until now how you felt about him. He might feel encouraged to speak to you, or even ask you out. You may feel that your parents are always blurting out the Wrong Thing at the Wrong Moment, but wait – it might *not* be the Wrong Moment, at all, and it might even turn out to be the Right Thing.

3) Of course, parents are bound to say the Wrong Thing at the Wrong Moment at some point in your life (or even more often than that). Don't despair. Be patient with them. A consoling thought is that your friends won't be paying that much attention, anyway, because they are all too busy trying to keep their own parents under control.

4) Admiring your work is an important part of any Open Day. All your best work has been put out on display.

• The scene
Mr and Mrs Average are in the school art room.

'Oh look, Kevin!' says Mrs Average to her husband. 'That must be one of Amy's paintings.' She points to a fantastic 'bird of paradise' design painted by one of the more talented members of the school. 'Is it one of yours, dear?'

'No, Mum, it isn't. This is one of mine.' Amy points to a rather strange pink and grey daub, which looks like some kind of shapeless, jelly thing, splodged on to paper.

'Oh.' Mr and Mrs Average stand in silence and 'admire' their daughter's work.

In order to avoid parental disappointment, gently guide your parents in the direction of what you know to be your best work, or alternatively guide them towards the school hall where refreshments are now being served.

5) Try to avoid impromptu parent/teacher consultations in front of your friends and your friends' parents:

• The scene

Mr and Mrs Toogood are drinking tea and eating biscuits in the school hall. Mr Toogood notices Angelica's maths teacher standing alone, and strides up to him, beaming with confidence:

'Good afternoon, Mr Featherwell. I must congratulate you!'(*Must* he?) 'Angelica has been making excellent progress in her biology studies this term, under your inspired and ever-watchful eye.' (What is he talking about?) 'Your guidance and tuition, and, I must say, abundant patience, have brought her on in leaps and bounds. She seems to take a particular interest in biology, especially human biology. Might she go in to study it at university level, do you think?'

'Actually, I teach maths. And the name's Tomkins.'

'Ah. Well, er, she's doing very well at maths, too.'

'No, she isn't.'

'Oh. Why's that?'

'She has no mathematical ability whatsoever, and no interest in the subject. I might as well bang my head repeatedly against a brick wall, as teach your daughter.'

'Oh. Do you think extra tuition would help?'

'No.'

Angelica notices that one of her father's friends is listening intently to this conversation. So it is not just

Angelica herself, but her father as well, who is likely to feel embarrassed by this unfortunate and ill-timed parent/teacher consultation.

If you are of the opinion that it would be better if your parent and your teachers did not 'consult' each other (or even 'insult' each other), think of a way of distracting your parents, and hauling them off in a different direction.

'Have you been to see the School Pond?' Angelica asks

her parents brightly. 'There are loads of frogs.' Mr and Mrs Toogood look slightly surprised by this sudden interest in pond life – but, on the other hand, their daughter is very keen on biology.

6) You may have to contend with the embarrassing tendency of parents to 'tidy you up' in public. They simply cannot resist turning your collar down, straightening your tie, combing your hair, tucking your shirt in, or just tucking a label in. They just *have* to flick dust (or dandruff?) off your jacket, or even (horror of horrors) spit on a handkerchief and polish your face with it. How do you stop them making you look about four years old in front of all your friends?

i) You make sure you are smart and thoroughly 'tucked-in' everywhere, that there is nothing left for them to do. The only trouble with this, of course, is that you end up looking a complete idiot, and the chances are they will *still* find the one button you missed doing up.

ii) You can have your revenge by tidying *them* up, straightening your father's tie and tucking a label inside your mother's dress collar. This is satisfying, but doesn't really solve the problem.

iii) You might like to consider that monkeys go in for mutual grooming in a social context, and we, as humans, are not that far removed. This is either a comforting or a worrying thought, depending on how fond you are of monkeys.

iv) All right. Admit it. There is no answer to this one. Sorry. It is another NYCDAI situation, and it is not really

a good idea to flinch away from whoever is 'tidying you up'. They mean well, and you will only hurt their feelings if you openly reject them. Try having a quiet word in private.

In public, it is best to maintain the united family front.

CHAPTER 4
Family Fun
(Family gatherings and how to survive them)

PROBLEM 1: Happy birthday to you

• The birthday scene - 1

Soumik's parents have arranged a family party to celebrate his fourteenth birthday. His Aunt Aneena brings a present, which Soumik unwraps in front of everyone – and then wishes he hadn't. It is a large, lavishly-illustrated book (it says on the cover that it is lavishly-illustrated) entitled *Body Facts – A Guide To How Your Body Works*.

'It is a most useful book,' says Aunt Aneena. 'And the illustrations are lavish, very lavish indeed. I have given a copy of this book to my girls also, because they were always asking questions. Now, when they ask me questions, I just tell them to go and look at the book. Yes, it is a most useful book. Useful for girls. Useful for a boy.'

Meanwhile, Soumik's girl cousins are rocking with barely suppressed laughter, and one of them explodes into a loud snigger, which sets off several others.

'What is so funny, may I ask?' Aunt Aneena demands. 'Be quiet, girls!'

So how do you react to the unwanted/unwelcome gift? The answer is, you should always say 'Thank you,'

and pretend that you are very pleased. It is just not worth causing offence by showing your true feelings. Anyway, if you seem grateful, the chances are that your relation will give you more presents in the future, which may be a lot better (or they may be worse).

• The birthday scene - 2
Danny really wants a new bike for his birthday, and an outing for himself and a few friends to the Hyper Bowl, followed by a slap-up meal at The Blue Porcupine.

• What he hopes his mother will say: 'Yes, darling. If that's what you want, of course you can have it.'

• What his mother will actually say: 'I'm sorry, darling, but you know we're broke. I can't possibly manage all of that. I was going to get you a smart pair of jeans, a

sweater and a shirt. Oh, and some socks and underpants.'

It is necessary to compromise: Mrs Broke has said that she can't manage *all* of what he wants, which means that she might be persuaded to manage some of it. If he can persuade her that he already has enough trousers, shirts, sweaters, socks, underpants, etc, ('Honestly, Mum, I think you've got enough things to wash and iron already!') then perhaps she will put the money towards a visit to the Hyper Bowl and The Blue Porcupine, instead. What would probably win her over completely would be if he asks her if she would come with him because he 'really enjoys her company' and he's 'really proud' that she's his mum. Perhaps he could take just one friend with him, as well, because his friends all like her as well – she's such fun. In fact, if he carries on being so irresistibly charming, the chances are that Mrs Broke will start saving like mad to get him the bike he wants, as well.

• The birthday scene - 3

A birthday in the Toogood household can mean only one thing – yet another extraordinary cake! Mrs Toogood bakes Angelica a Giant Banana Buttercreamfly Cake, one of her specialities, with apricot and almond glaze. And 'glazed' is how people tend to look after eating it. But Angelica thanks her mother very much, and says how delicious the cake looks, far too good to eat, so can they wait till her friends arrive so they can all see it before it gets eaten?

'What friends?' asks Mrs Toogood, unaware that her daughter has invited everyone.

'It's a surprise party!' replies Angelica.

'Yes, but … shouldn't it be someone else who's surprising you?' ventures Mrs Toogood. 'Can you really give yourself a "surprise party"?'

'Oh,' says Angelica, looking crestfallen. 'But you'll still let me have the party, won't you? I mean, it's my birthday, and everything.'

Angelica has worked out the Really Useful Thing about birthdays. You can do whatever you want (almost) and, if anyone challenges you or tries to stop you, you just say, 'But it's my birthday!' in a hurt and injured tone of voice. Whoever it is will then feel guilty, and let you carry on with whatever it is.

So Angelica has her 'surprise party'. She is holding the party in her bedroom, so she can try out the new stereo sound system with built-in flashing lights (like Sam's) which she has successfully persuaded her parents to give her for her birthday. She has invited four girls from her class, including Amy, plus Danny, and another guy from school called Jez. She is not normally allowed boys in the bedroom (ever since the Sam episode), so her birthday has given her the ideal excuse for breaking a few house rules. But she should beware of breaking too many. Because tomorrow is not her birthday.

PROBLEM 2: A family wedding

• The scene - 1
Going to buy that special outfit

Angelica's mother and her Aunty Glenda take her to buy a special outfit to wear at Aunty Glenda's wedding (Aunty Glenda is to marry Uncle Norman, with whom she has been living for the past twelve years). They go to Horrids department store and have a Horridburger in the Rooftop Restaurant before going to the Horrid Dress Department. Angelica notices a very attractive boy standing nearby, waiting while a rather pretty girl (Angelica hopes it might be his sister) is trying on some clothes. Angelica thinks he might be looking at her. Mrs Toogood and Aunty Glenda choose this moment to select a *dreadful frock* (the Frock from Hell), and hold it up against her. It is bright blue and orange, with a huge floral pattern, gold buttons and a pleated skirt which goes down to her ankles. It is made from shiny nylon, and it makes Angelica look about ninety-four years old.

THE FROCK FROM HELL

Her friends would die laughing if they saw her in it. She would just *die*. The good-looking guy isn't looking at her any more. He has wandered off. She doesn't blame him.

'Angel, darling, you look *sweet!*' says Mrs Toogood.

'Go and try it on. You're a size ten, aren't you? Or maybe a size twelve?'

'I should say a size fourteen, dear,' says Aunty Glenda, in a loud voice, clearly audible throughout the whole of Horrids. 'She's getting quite a big girl now, isn't she?'

Suddenly Angelica feels *enormous*, like a barrage balloon. She *must* go on a diet.

What should Angelica do next?

• **The wrong thing to say:** 'If you think I'm going to wear this dress, you must be out of your tiny minds. I wouldn't be seen *dead* in it.'

• **The right thing to say:** 'It's very nice,' (through gritted teeth). If you pretend you like the awful clothes your parent or other relation has selected, they will be so delighted that they will probably agree to buy you something that *you* want. A wedding is always a good excuse for some new clothes, and you may be lucky – your parent may have excellent taste. Don't forget to mention that you need new shoes, a jacket, tights (well, not if you're a boy), maybe a hat. But don't expect them to buy you a new pair of trainers with Advanced Power Soles to go to a wedding.

• **The scene – 2**
At the reception

Angelica finds that all her relations and family friends are at the wedding. The reception is held at a hotel, where everyone stands around drinking champagne and admiring the cake, which has been made by Mrs Toogood. They admire the bride, the bridesmaids, the flowers, each others' hats, and anything else they can find. They even admire Angelica, who thinks she will go mad if yet another relation comes up to her and asks her the same questions, always starting with the same opening remark: 'Goodness me, you've grown! How's school? You must be coming up for GCSEs, aren't you? Have you decided what you want to do when you leave school?' There is so much general background noise, chat and laughter, that they can't even hear Angelica's answers anyway, and soon lose interest and wander away.

Angelica has one glass of champagne, and notices suddenly, to her surprise, that the floor is on a slope, and that it keeps tilting from side to side. At the same time she realises that the best man is the most gorgeous guy she has ever set eyes on, and she must go immediately and tell him straight out how much she fancies him.

• What Angelica hopes the best man will say: 'Wow! You're beautiful! Where have you been all my life? Let me take you away from all this, in my sports car.'

• What the best man actually says: 'Hello, you must be Angelica. Goodness me, how you've grown! How's school? You must be coming up for GCSEs. What do you want to do when you leave school? Oh dear, are you all right? Here, let me get you a chair.'

The best Angelica can hope for is not the best man, but that she is *not* seated next to Uncle Kevin when they go in for the wedding sit-down meal. Uncle Kevin has had far more champagne than she has, and thinks, wrongly, that he is totally irresistible to every female in the room.

Here are some other ideas for surviving the wedding reception:

1) If it is held at an hotel, you can go exploring. The ladies' room is usually a relatively quiet place where you can have a chat with one of the friendlier guests, and try out the little soaps and bottles of hand cream, etc. (But not if you're a bloke.)

2) All your relations and family friends will be at the reception. Be prepared for them all to say the same things and ask the same questions. You could always write down the answers on the back of a menu card:

Then, when you see Aunty Pat or Uncle Harold (have you noticed you can have an 'aunty' but not an 'uncly'?) bearing down on you with a huge smile and 'Angelica! Darling! How you've grown ...' etc, you can simply hold up your card. They will peer at it short-sightedly (too much champagne, perhaps), give you a funny look, and then, with any luck, they will go away and leave you alone.

3) If you just want to escape, you can pretend to feel faint, or even stage a dramatic passing-out-completely-on-the-floor (depending on how much of an actor you are). Lots of kind people will immediately come to your assistance, with remarks like: 'It's his/her age, you know,' 'Poor thing!', 'It is terribly hot in here, isn't it?' With any luck, you may even find yourself taken to one of the hotel rooms to lie down, with TV, own bathroom, coffee-making equipment, etc.

PROBLEM 3: Festive fun – it's Christmas!

• The Christmas scene

The Toogood family is preparing for the festive season. Becky has turned into a one-girl paper chain factory, Mr Toogood is trying unsuccessfully to get the Christmas tree lights to work, and Mrs Toogood is hard at work in the kitchen, churning out more and more mince pies, an enormous Christmas pudding which is so alcoholic that it immediately catches fire when someone strikes a match several feet away, and the most elaborate Christmas angel cake that ever was (it is beautifully iced, and there are so many little snowman decorations, little Christmas trees, Father Christmases, reindeer, etc, on top of it that they are beginning to fall off the edges).

The house is filled with a warm, spicy smell from the mulled wine which Grant is preparing (he really lets rip at Christmas time). So why doesn't it feel like Christmas?

Angelica shuts herself in her room, and feels miserable. She doesn't know why. How can she beat those Christmas blues ('I'm dreaming of a blue Christmas … ')? Here are some thoughts which may or may not spread a little seasonal warmth and good cheer:

1) Make a wonderful Christmas card and give it to the boy/girl you have secretly fancied like mad for a long time. Christmas, like Valentine's Day, gives you a good excuse to do things you wouldn't normally do (give cards, presents, kisses, hugs, etc), and say things you wouldn't normally say ('Happy Christmas').

2) Make a long list for Father Christmas of all the amazing and expensive things you desperately want (new iPod, CD-DVD burner, cool trainers with Super Advanced Power Soles, snowboard, mountain bike and so on).

Again, Christmas gives you a good excuse to do things like this. You probably won't get all the things on your list, but, if your dad wins the lottery, at least he will know what to do with the money.

3) Make a more realistic list of all the useful things you really need (new pen, folders, etc, for school, underwear – or just money). Give this to your parent so that he or she knows what to say when all your relations ask what you want for Christmas. Unfortunately, of course, they very often don't ask. They just give you a book token.

4) The thought of being stuck with your family for

several days, having to be 'jolly', and feeling over-stuffed (like the turkey), is probably enough to make anyone feel depressed, so plan a few escape routes:

i) Arrange to go 'carol-singing' with a few friends one evening. This means that you can go to the house of the boy/girl that you really fancy, and sing to them. In order to stop you singing, the boy/girl of your dreams might invite you into their house, and who knows what this may lead to ...

ii) Have an alternative Christmas in your room, with a few friends (or just one friend), and listen to music (probably not *Jingle Bells* or *Rudolph the Red-nosed Reindeer*).

iii) Get a good supply of magazines before the festive season gets seriously underway.

iv) Go out for plenty of walks and fresh air. Anyway, you will want to try out your new mountain bike, skateboard, etc.

v) You will probably get invited to all sorts of houses for various parties, and, no matter how boring it may seem at first, you never know, there may be someone at one of these parties who feels the same way as you (almost certainly there is). Keep an open mind. You never know whom you might meet ...

vi) Carry some mistletoe with you at all times, in case you see the boy/girl of your dreams. Then you can hold the mistletoe above your head, pucker up and wait ... (This is what Angelica did.)

A FESTIVE PROBLEM

• The scene

Danny is not sure how to be in two places at once. He would like to spend Christmas with his mother. He would also like to spend Christmas with his father. Unfortunately, his mother and father live in different houses, a fair distance apart. Even if he gets the

Supersonic Skateboard he wants for Christmas, he is still going to have his work cut out, zipping from one house to the other, and is likely to end up with indigestion (even worse than the usual Christmas indigestion) after eating two Christmas dinners (turkey times two – gobble, gobble.)

So what can he do?

• **Answer:** He cannot be in two places at once. This is not a terribly helpful answer. So, what else can he do?

If your parents are halfway sensible, they will have worked it all out for you. They will suggest that you spend one Christmas with one parent, and the next Christmas with the other parent, and so on. You will be treated like a seasonal ping-pong ball, but never mind. It could be worse.

Let's look at how it could be worse.

Danny's mum and dad have left the ball (the ping-pong ball) firmly in Danny's court. It is up to him to choose where he wants to be at Christmas. He is worried about upsetting either his mother or father.

Actually, it shouldn't be such a problem. Let's face it – Christmas goes on a bit. It is not just one day. There is Christmas Eve, Christmas Day, Boxing Day and loads of other days either side. Danny could spend some of the festive season with one parent, and the rest with the other. He may even do quite well out of this, ending up having two major Christmas celebrations, whereas most people make do with just one.

Here are a few points to consider:

1) Get your parents to book well ahead if they require your company on a certain day. Indicate to them that you are much in demand. They will be impressed (or irritated).

2) Christmas can be a stressful time for any family. Get a good supply of magazines, books, favourite music, etc, and find a place to escape to (the bathroom?).

3) 'Tis the season of peace and good will to all men!' Says who?

CHAPTER 5

Holidays

PROBLEM 1: Where to go on holiday

• The scene - 1

Angelica wants to go for a fortnight to sun-drenched Tenerife, where she can lie by the pool, get a really good suntan and make loads of new friends (or maybe just one incredibly handsome friend). The rest of the Toogood family is planning the usual fortnight away in Llandiddly-upon-Sea in North Wales, where they have been every summer for the last fifteen years.

• What Angelica hopes her parents will say: 'Yes, Angel, of course you can go to Tenerife. We'll pay for you to go there on your own, and the rest of us will go to Llandiddly.'

• What Angelica's parents actually say: 'I hardly think Tenerife is a suitable place. It's full of tourists and foreigners – and terribly hot.'

• The best that Angelica can hope for: If she leaves tempting-looking brochures of sun-drenched Tenerife and other resorts around the house, she may sow the seeds of a new idea in her parents' mind. 'I suppose it is a bit boring going to Llandiddly year after year,' says Mrs Toogood, as though this thought has only just

occurred to her (fifteen years later). 'Perhaps we should try somewhere different this year?'

'Good idea,' agrees Mr Toogood, getting out his A–Z roadmap of Britain. 'How about Cornwall?' This is *slightly* nearer to Tenerife than North Wales, but not *quite* the same, somehow. Angelica can now try another tactic: 'My teacher says it's really important as part of the National Curriculum in the run-up to GCSEs, that we should go abroad somewhere, and experience different cultures.'

'Hmm ...' says Mr Toogood, going to the bookcase and getting out a very out-of-date roadmap of Europe. 'I suppose we could motor through France ... and we might even reach Italy.' He is getting quite excited, now. So you may not get to quite where you want. But you can probably get to somewhere *different*.

• The scene - 2

Danny Broke really wants to go to the Caribbean where his best mate is going to do loads of glamorous water sports. Mrs Broke wants to visit Wales and explore the countryside.

• What Danny hopes his mother will say:

'Yes, darling, if that's what you want, of course we'll go.'

• What Mrs Broke will actually say: 'You

know I'm broke so you'll have to make do with Wales.' They go to deepest Wales and meet a lot of sheep.

• The best that Danny can hope for: He sug-

gests they rent a cottage near the sea. Mrs Broke is too broke to rent a cottage, so they take a tent. They pitch their tent just outside Llandiddly-upon-Sea, which has a windsurfing centre and a swimming complex called Waterfun, where there is a big waterchute to slide down into a nearly Olympic-size pool. There is also plenty of surrounding countryside and sheep to please his mother. This is not quite what he had in mind but, again, it's ... different.

PROBLEM 2: How to get to take what you want

• The scene

Angelica has piled everything she wants to take with her on holiday on top of the bed. There is a change of clothes for every day (fourteen changes of clothes), three pairs of pyjamas and some of her smartest and sexiest items of clothing for evening-wear (six additional skirts, tops and dresses), four bikinis, twenty pairs of knickers, seven bras, ten pairs of tights, one hairdrier, three wash-bags bulging with shampoo, conditioner, cleanser, toner, moisturiser, suntan cream, make-up, make-up remover, cotton wool, hairbrush, and so on. There is also her favourite teddy bear, some magazines, camera, diary, iPod, photo of boyfriend (Sam doesn't know she took it) and her football. And six pairs of shoes and sandals.

• What Angelica hopes her mother will say: 'I'll fetch you another suitcase, Angel, and shall I help you pack? I'll sit on the suitcase for you while you lock it.'

• What Angelica's mother actually says: 'You can't possibly take all of that! We haven't got room in the car. The boot's already full with all your brother's moth-collecting equipment, and we still have to get the picnic chairs and picnic table on the roof rack.'

I HAVEN'T GOT A THING TO WEAR!

• **A different approach which might get you more of what you really want to take with you:** Angelica does *not* pile all her clothes and things on the bed. Instead, she sits on an empty bed and looks fed-up. 'What's the matter?' asks her mother. 'I haven't really got anything to take,' she says. 'I haven't got a thing to wear. I've grown out of everything. I've got nothing smart for the evenings, all my tights have got holes in, and I've lost my most comfortable bra. And my sandals are hurting me. And my trainers are falling to bits.

I can't go on holiday!' She bursts into tears. 'There, there!' says Mrs Toogood. 'Cheer up, Angel, we'll go shopping, shall we, and get you what you need?' (YESSS!)

PROBLEM 3: How to get what you want during the day (and get out of what you don't want)

• The holiday scene – 1

The Toogood family has reached Amiens in France. They have found a very pleasant small hotel to stay in. Mr and Mrs Toogood have finished their croissants, and are keen to visit the cathedral. Mr Toogood wants to try out his French on the unsuspecting locals. Grant and Angelica find this embarrassing, as their father seems to think that if he speaks French in a very loud voice, they will understand what he is saying. But Angelica notices that people start laughing, and some of them even make a little gesture which indicates that they think Mr Toogood is mad. So she and her brother and Becky are keen to go in a different direction. They would like to sit at a pavement café and drink *café au lait*, or *citron pressé*. Angelica and Becky can then keep a look-out for hunky French boys, and Grant can read his book in peace.

• What Angelica hopes her parents will say: 'Yes, of course, Angel, off you go and enjoy yourselves. We'll be all right.'

• **What Mr and Mrs Toogood actually say:** 'But you can't possibly come all the way to Amiens and not visit the cathedral! Come along, now, let's all keep together, shall we?'

• **The best she can hope for:** Angelica can always say she has a headache and would like to sit quietly somewhere. 'How about that nice café under the big trees in the square outside our hotel? Becky, Grant and I will just sit there and wait for you. Anyway, you and Dad deserve some time on your own together, without us. This could be your second honeymoon, you know? Go and enjoy yourselves!'

Angelica notices that her mother is quite taken with this idea. 'Well, if you're sure you'll be all right ... but make sure you stay exactly where you are.'

Staying exactly where she is, as far as Angelica is concerned, is preferable to hearing her father's very bad French echoing around Amiens cathedral.

• **The holiday scene – 2**
Mrs Broke has picked up a leaflet from the Llandiddly Tourist Information Kiosk, detailing places to visit around Llandiddly. There is an ancient hill fort which is not too far away, and she suggests to Danny that they go and visit it, and take a picnic. This sounds deadly dull, and Danny is keen to get back to the Waterfun centre, where he has already made a few friends. These friends told him on good authority that Waterfun is the only place in or around Llandiddly which is not totally dead.

There is *nowhere* worth visiting, unless you are a sheep, or about ninety years old.

• What Danny hopes Mrs Broke will say:
'OK, darling, you go and enjoy yourself at Waterfun, and I'll go to the Llandiddly-upon-Sea Ancient Hill Fort on my own.'

• **What Mrs Broke actually says:** 'But, dar-ling, what are you going to do about lunch? I can't really have a picnic on my own. I've hardly seen anything of you since we got here.' (Doesn't she see enough of him when they're at home?)

• **Time for a compromise:** Danny suggests to his mother that if they go their separate ways during the day, they could meet up in the evening and go for a nice long walk together round Llandiddly and then go up on to the hill where they've pitched their tent, for an evening picnic. 'I'd really enjoy that,' says Danny. 'It would be something to look forward to at the end of the day.' Once again, his incredible charm wins his mother over com-pletely. 'And,' says Danny, 'you can tell me all about the hill fort. It sounds fascinating.'

This approach is much more likely to succeed than the 'God, I don't want to do *that*. It sounds *boring*,' approach.

PROBLEM 4: How to be allowed out in the evenings to meet some other teenagers/gorgeous waiter

• **The scene – 1**

The Toogood family has made it to Italy. Angelica is in the back of the car, drooling out of the window at all the fab-ulous Italian boys, who are inclined to drool back at her.

'Why do those boys keep staring at us?' says Mr Toogood.

'Look, he's sticking his tongue out and waggling it at us!' says Mrs Toogood. 'How rude!'

'It's been a long drive,' says Mr Toogood, changing the subject. 'We'd better all have an early night. Ah, here's our hotel.'

Angelica has arranged to meet Giovanni the gorgeous waiter in the town square that evening. There is to be a floodlit show in the square for the tourists so she hopes to use this as an excuse to escape.

• **What Angelica hopes her parents will say:** 'Of course, Angel, you go and watch the show. Your father and I are tired. We'll go to bed early.'

• **What Angelica's parents actually say:** 'Oh yes, that sounds fun! Let's all go to the show!'

• **The best she can hope for:** There is quite a crowd in the town square, so she manages to slip away

from her parents, and meet Giovanni in a quiet corner. Unfortunately, one of the spotlights swings round and she finds her first kiss with Giovanni spectacularly illuminated to a great burst of applause, cheers and wolf-whistles from the assembled crowd. Mr and Mrs Toogood, she notices, are *not* clapping. However, at least she got to see him – briefly.

• The scene - 2

Danny wants to escape from the tent and his mother on Llandiddly Hill, and go back into town on his own to meet up with his friends from Waterfun. There is a group of girls whom they might get to know, and walk around town with.

• What Danny hopes his mother will say:

'Yes, darling, of course. Off you go. I'll be all right.'

• What Mrs Broke actually says: 'Well, I'm

not staying up here on my own.' (Actually, they are in a field packed with tents and caravans, but, apparently this is not enough for her.) 'Tell you what,' she continues, 'we could go on a night-time mackerel fishing expedition! I saw a notice about it – the next boat leaves harbour at eight p.m. We'll just make it. Come on!' So once again, Danny's life seems destined to revolve around fish. (Llandiddly smoked mackerel are famous, and Mrs Broke sells them at the fish shop.)

• The best he can hope for: There is another

teenage boy on the boat, and he and Danny become friends. It is not quite the sort of evening he had in mind, but they do catch a lot of mackerel.

You cannot blame your parents for not wanting to let you out of their sight in the evening. There are a lot of dodgy people out there, even in Llandiddly (especially in Llandiddly). It is better to go out in the company of an elder sibling (a big brother is ideal), or at least with some friends your parents already know and like. Always say what time you'll be back, *and make sure you are*. Tell them *where* you are going. If you're on holiday somewhere, there's usually some fun but fairly safe place to go (flood-lit dry ski slope/bowling/cinema/ice-rink, etc) or organised event (even if it's just a game of football on the campsite). Show them how responsible you are, and they'll let you out again.

By the way, a word of advice: it is probably *not* a good idea to make long phone calls home to your boyfriend/girlfriend, at your parents' expense, especially if you are abroad. This sort of behaviour is likely to contribute to 'holiday stress'. A postcard will do.

PROBLEM 5: Coping with holiday stress

• The scene

The Toogood family are on their way home. Mr Toogood is tired and has spent more money than he intended. Mrs Toogood has lost her handbag somewhere in Italy, and is in a state of profound panic. Grant is permanently grumbling about how uncomfortable he is in the back of the car, and he is covered in mosquito bites. Becky is car-sick, and they have to keep stopping, which is difficult on the motorway. Angelica is distraught because she has had to leave the gorgeous waiter behind, and her suntan is beginning to peel and itch. Basically, they have all had *enough*.

So how do you cope with it all?

1) Put on your iPod, but not too loud, otherwise the just audible 'sst sst sst' noise will cause further stress to the other members of your family.

2) You can escape into a daydream about the gorgeous waiter/waitress, and how things might have been.

3) Instead of escaping into a world of your own, it might be more to your advantage to come back down to earth and think about the other members of your family for a moment. They are all feeling a little exhausted and stressed. Why not say, suddenly, 'Hey, Mum and Dad, thanks for a really great holiday! You're the best, you know. I really enjoyed the whole thing. Let's do it again some time?' They may be quite taken aback by this spontaneous outburst of affection and gratitude, but the knowledge you have enjoyed the holiday they went to a certain amount of trouble and expense to organise, will go quite a long way towards de-stressing them. (Instead of 'distressed', they will be feeling 'de-stressed'.) In fact, showing them your appreciation in this way will make them more inclined in the future to take you on holiday again, this time, maybe where *you* want to go.

4) Bear in mind that the days of family holidays are numbered, unless you intend to live at home until you are forty, or even older. This is another reason why you should do your best to enjoy what is good about them, and show your appreciation.

5) And if it is all too much for you, take a deep breath, count to ten, then burst into tears.

6) When you arrive home, you all need time and space to chill out, so go straight to the 'De-stressing Chamber' (your own room) and relax. Put on some music, unpack, think about how you will soon be seeing your friends again, including the boy or girl in your class at school whom you fancy like mad. And admit it ...

IT'S GOOD TO BE HOME.

More brilliant books by Kathryn Lamb

ACCORDING TO ALEX
The World According to Alex
The Last Word According to Alex
For Better or Worse According to Alex
Summer, Sun and Stuff According to Alex

BEST MATES FOREVER (BMF)
Love, Mates and Money
Vices and Virtues
Brothers, Boyfriends and Babe Magnets

Honestly Mum!

☆

www.piccadillypress.co.uk

☆ The latest news on forthcoming books

☆ Chapter previews

☆ Author biographies

☆ Fun quizzes

☆ Reader reviews

☆ Competitions and fab prizes

☆ Book features and cool downloads

☆ And much, much more . . .

Log on and check it out!

Piccadilly Press